Chris C. Pinney, D.V.M.

Dachshunds

Everything About Purchase, Care, Nutrition, and Beh...

Fille... ...graphs
Illus... ...e-Bridges

BARRON'S

CONTENTS

AN INTRODUCTION TO THE DACHSHUND

In 1839, the second year of the reign of Her Majesty Queen Victoria, a dashing visitor appeared in the inner circles of the English Royal Court. Bold, outspoken, and affectionate, he quickly won the favor of his new monarch and proceeded to take it upon himself to assume the role of her chief protector. His brave and courageous demeanor impressed those around him, and his loyalty to Crown was never in question. Yet, while other subjects could earn a quick trip to the Tower of London for being obstinate and ill-tempered in the presence of their sovereign, he alone was immune to such punishment. In fact, when feeling especially bellicose, he might even get away with soiling the Royal Rug a time or two! His name was Dachsy. And the secret to his success was a cute face, eager eyes, an adorable personality, and a funny-looking body. He was, indeed, the first Royal Dachshund.

Thank goodness you don't have to be royalty to reap the benefits that this unique and remarkable breed has to offer. Highly intelligent and loving, Dachshunds have secured their place in the hearts of millions worldwide. The Dachshund personality is certainly one of the most unique you will ever encounter. These happy, playful, and funny dogs can be extremely goal-oriented, feisty, and focused

Dachshunds are highly intelligent dogs.

when they put their mind to it. Keep this in mind when you begin your training sessions with your new Dachshund and learn to recognize and take into consideration this strong personality trait (see Training Your Dachshund, page 37). As a group, Dachshunds are good, even-tempered dogs that rank about average—exhibiting no glaring character flaws—when compared to other breeds in terms of trainability, excitability, playfulness, and interaction with children.

A Brief History of the Dachshund

As the Germanic name implies, the Dachshund (translated "badger dog") originated in Germany over 400 years ago. Some debate still exists regarding such origins, with many believing the breed is much older than this. Stone etchings and statues, thousands of years old and bearing a striking resemblance to the contemporary Dachshund, have been found in and about Egypt, Central America, South America, and China. In addition, remains of Dachshund-like canines have been found among ancient Roman settlements in Germany. There is no doubt that a dog closely resembling the Dachshund existed on earth in millennia past; but the dog that we know and love today is the result of selective crossbreeding by German hunters in sixteenth-century Europe. These hunters were looking for a dog that would "go to earth" against a popular quarry of that day, the badger. Owing to the fierce and fiery disposition of the badger, the dog chosen to follow such a quarry into its burrow had to possess a pugnacious and fearless spirit, as well as the anatomical build to perform the task with efficiency. In the Dachshund, these Teutonic hunters got this and a whole lot more. Not only was this dog used to root badgers, fox, and rabbits out of their dens and subsequently subdue them—their low center of gravity was ideal for stability during the fight—but used in packs they could even chase and track larger quarry, such as deer and boar, over vast distances, despite their shortened appendages. They proved to be excellent watchdogs at home as well, equipped with a keen sense of hearing and a loud, shrill bark that served as an efficient alarm system.

Coat Variety

Today's Dachshund can trace its ancestry back to old German hunting dogs and various short-legged terrier types found in Germany at that time. The first Dachshunds were of the smooth-haired variety, with a short, dense coat, and weighing in around 30 to 35 pounds (14–16 kg). Later, variations appeared through selective breeding. For instance, long-haired Dachshunds, possessing a soft, wavy coat, were developed by crossing smooth-haired members of the breed with field spaniels and other breeds of gundog, including the German Stoeber. In the wire-haired, hunters and breeders saw the need to develop a variety with a wiry, tough coat that could withstand the rigors of hunting in thick brush and thorns. By crossing smooth-haired

varieties with wire-coated terriers, this aim was achieved. Later, Schnauzers, Dandie Dinmont Terriers, and others were used as outcrosses to firm up the quality of this Dachshund variety.

Size

Coat length wasn't the only feature that early breeders chose to address. The size of the final product was seen as an important variable closely related to function. For this reason, today we find Dachshunds of different sizes. Standard Dachshunds may range anywhere from 16 to 32 pounds (7–14 kg), whereas those considered miniatures typically weigh less than 11 pounds (5 kg). Hunters wanted smaller dogs that could easily enter the lairs of smaller game, such as rabbits. With this end in mind, a reduction in the size of the breed was obtained years ago by crossing the smaller Dachshunds then in existence with small terriers and pinschers. Even the size of these new miniatures would vary. For example, though most tipped the scales at around 10 pounds (4.5 kg), miniature Dachshunds weighing no more than 5 pounds (2 kg) were favorites among European rabbit hunters during the first decades of the twentieth century.

Breed Recognition

As far as a timeline for breed recognition is concerned, the first edition of the *Deutscher Hunde-Stammbuch*, published in 1840, contained over 50 registered Dachshunds. However, official standards for the breed weren't established in Germany until 1879. Nine years later, the Deutscher Teckel Klub was created in Berlin to maintain these standards and to organize bench trials for the breed. Around the same time, Gebrauchsteckel Klubs (Hunting

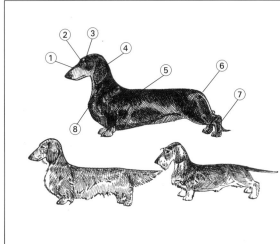

Illustrated Breed Standard

1. Fine, slightly arched muzzle
2. Little perceptible stop
3. Almond-shaped eyes
4. High-set, rounded ears
5. Back straight and long
6. Tail set as a continuation of the topline
7. Legs short
8. Breastbone strongly prominent

❏ **Color:** solid red, sable, or cream; black and tan, chocolate and tan, wild boar and tan, gray and tan, or fawn and tan; single dapple (lighter color set on darker background, as in a merle); double dapple (white in addition to dapple); brindle

❏ **DQ:** knuckled over

*DQ = disqualification

Dachshund Associations) began to appear with the purpose of promoting the function of the Dachshund more than its form. These associations organized hunting trials and events, and even kept separate stud books from those kept by the Deutscher Teckel Klub. It was not until 1935 that the clubs united efforts in the common purpose of promoting the breed.

Although Dachshunds had no doubt made their way across the English Channel prior to the coronation of Queen Victoria, it was certainly her attraction to the breed and the interest exhibited by her subjects that eventually led to the Dachshund being awarded breed status in England in 1873. In 1881 the English Dachshund Club was chartered, with the duty of advancing the breed throughout the British Isles. Today, the Dachshund is one of the most popular dogs in Britain.

Dachshunds began to appear in the United States in the late nineteenth century, with the first recorded dog, a smooth-haired, medium-size individual, imported in 1870 by a Dr. Twadell of Philadelphia, Pennsylvania. In 1895 the Dachshund Club of America was formed to help promote the breed in the United States. Although the ancestors of today's American lines were introduced into the United States for the purpose of hunting rabbits and other small burrowing game, their role soon evolved over the years from hunter to house pet. The notoriety of Dachshunds as a house pet suffered during the early and mid-twentieth century due to war-induced prejudice, but following World War II, their popularity began to grow again. Today, they are among the top ten most popular breeds registered by the American Kennel Club.

THE DECISION TO OWN A DACHSHUND

Although Dachshunds were originally developed for hunting, years of domestication have produced an outstanding house pet. Highly affectionate and loving dogs, they quickly form close bonds with their owners and are clean and easy to maintain. Their size makes them ideal for apartment dwellers and those with limited living space. Smart and relatively easy to house-train, they can quickly become adjusted to almost any living environment.

However, prior to making the commitment to purchase a Dachshund, there are several questions you need to ask yourself and, in turn, feel very comfortable with your answers.

✔ Why do I want a Dachshund in the first place?
✔ What type of Dachshund do I really want?
✔ Do I want a puppy or a more mature dog?
✔ Do I want a male or female Dachshund?
✔ How will my children (if applicable) be affected by my new Dachshund?
✔ Do I have other pets in the household that will be affected by this new addition?
✔ Am I willing to accept the financial and time responsibility associated with Dachshund ownership?
✔ Am I willing to house my Dachshund indoors?

By satisfactorily addressing these issues ahead of time, you can spare yourself unex-

Before purchasing a Dachshund, be sure to fully understand the role that it will play in your family.

pected surprises and regrets, knowing that you have indeed made the correct decision prior to bringing your new friend home.

Your Dachshund's Role

The Dachshund is a fun-loving breed that is capable of exhibiting lots of love, affection, loyalty, and spunk. As a result, it is capable of filling many roles as a pet. You must recognize which role(s) you expect yours to play.

As a companion, it is hard to find one as much fun and fulfilling as the Dachshund. Equipped with a lively, playful personality, these dogs are as devoted as they come. Although they can experience their share of bouts of stubbornness, as alluded to earlier, they make loyal and affectionate pets.

As one might expect, anatomical limitations certainly exclude several types of owner-pet activities for the Dachshund—such as that 5-mile (9 km) jog with you—but don't be fooled. Keep in mind the ancestral genes in each and every Dachshund; they have tremendous strength and stamina, and if they could keep up with you, they could no doubt complete the route with wind to spare. Dachshunds are bursting with energy and love to play, and if you can keep up with them, they will provide you with an active source of fun, exercise, and interaction every day.

The Dachshund's warm disposition and medium-size frame makes it an excellent choice for households with children. It is extremely important to remember, however, that due to the predisposition of the breed to back injuries, children must be taught the proper rules concerning lifting and playing with Dachshunds to prevent inadvertent injury.

As a protector, the Dachshund is stalwart and courageous, not hesitating to throw itself into harm's way to protect a loved one. Exhibiting a keen sense of smell—thanks to its hound ancestry—and hearing, it can sense a stranger approaching long before he arrives. This, coupled with a natural cleverness and curiosity makes the Dachshund hard to fool.

Competition

You can be sure that the Dachshund's intelligence, looks, and strong will make it a formidable competitor. Many Dachshunds naturally seem to enjoy the competitive environment the show ring has to offer, exhibiting marked determination and tenacity. And competitive events certainly afford you the chance to enhance your relationship with your dog. American Kennel Club (AKC) licensed events are regularly held across the country. These events are open to dogs over six months of age and registered with the American Kennel Club. Locations of activities in your area can be traced through your local newspapers and pet periodicals, breeders, veterinarians, trainers, and dog clubs. You can also contact the AKC directly for listings of competitions in your locale, or better yet, consider subscribing to *The AKC Gazette*, available through the AKC, for complete listings of events throughout the country. A wealth of information can also be searched and retrieved via the Internet concerning competitions for your Dachshund (see The Competitive Dachshund, page 94).

Types of Dachshunds

In the United States, there are six varieties of Dachshunds to choose from: standard and miniature smooth-haired, standard and miniature long-haired, and standard and miniature wire-haired. Standard Dachshunds are those dogs weighing in excess of 16 pounds (7 kg); miniatures weigh less than 11 pounds (5 kg) at one year of age. Smooth-haired Dachshunds have short, dense, glossy coats that are velvety to the touch. Long-haired Dachshunds sport long, soft, sleek, and slightly wavy coats. Wire-haired varieties possess short, thick, coarse coats with dense undercoats. Obviously, both long-haired and wire-haired Dachshunds require greater attention to daily grooming than do their smooth-haired peers in order to keep their haircoats healthy and luxurious.

Believe it or not, coat length and body size may have a direct influence on the temperament and personality of a particular individual. For example, many Dachshund aficionados believe that the smooth-coated Dachshund tends to be more of a one-owner dog, exhibiting a greater degree of independence and territoriality. Long-haired Dachshunds are also described as being independent and somewhat reserved around strangers, whereas wire-haired Dachshunds are thought to be the most playful and outgoing of the three coat types. Finally, standard Dachshunds tend to be less nervous, less aggressive, and more trainable than their miniature counterparts.

In addition to varying coat lengths, Dachshunds come in all sorts of colors and patterns, including reds, shaded reds, chocolates, black and tans, brindles (equal mixture of black hairs and hairs of a lighter color throughout the coat), and dapples (silver, chocolate, or red base color, mixed with black and white hairs). The decision about which color or pattern strikes your fancy the most is strictly one of personal choice.

Factors to Consider When Choosing a Dachshund

Puppy or Adult?

The decision about whether or not to purchase a puppy or adult dog is again strictly your preference. There are many adult Dachshunds that have ended up in shelters and pounds simply because their owners could not care for them properly. They are just begging for a good, loving home. The advantage, of course, of choosing a more mature Dachshund is that you miss the trial and tribulations associated with puppyhood including chewing, biting, and house-training. Many adult Dachshunds are fully trained when you get them, which saves you a tremendous amount of time and effort. Also, an adult dog that has been properly cared for should be current on its immunizations, thus saving you the costs associated with a series of puppy checkups and shots.

Obviously, the disadvantage of choosing an adult dog is that training—including house-training—may never have been accomplished, or worse yet, the Dachshund may never have been properly socialized to other pets and/or people. Also, a personality or health defect may have prompted the previous owner to relinquish the dog. As a result, be sure to obtain as much information as you can regarding the dog's past, and request an in-home test period prior to making a full-fledged commitment to adopt such a dog.

The advantage of purchasing a puppy instead of an adult is that you have a chance to form a stronger, more emotional bond with your dog. Puppies between the ages of three and twelve weeks of age are in their peak period of socialization and readily form these bonds. They are also quite responsive to any training they are given during this time.

Male or Female?

The decision concerning the sex of your new Dachshund is again a matter of personal preference, as both males and females make excellent pets. Male dogs can be quite territorial and protective, whereas females are often thought to be more affectionate and trainable; however, there are multiple exceptions to this rule. Such qualities will vary in individual dogs and individual pedigrees, and will also be influenced by levels of training. Keep in mind that intact male dogs

TIP

Jumping

Dachshunds are notorious jumpers and will not hesitate to leap from great heights. Unfortunately, their anatomy does not lend well to such acrobatics, and serious back injuries can result. For this reason, it is vital that you train your Dachshund to stay off the furniture.

As companions, Dachshunds are as devoted as they come!

may also become quite restless and excited if there is a female dog in heat anywhere in your neighborhood. Often, they may dig a hole in the yard or squeeze through a hole in the fence in order to go looking for an opportunity. Intact female dogs will come into heat approximately twice a year, which often leads to a plethora of rogue male neighborhood dogs congregating around your house. Of course, one option is to neuter your pet at an early age. Not only will this procedure solve most of the problems mentioned above, but it will also prevent a number of serious diseases and disorders (see Neutering Your Dachshund, page 68).

Your Dachshund and Children

Before bringing an adult Dachshund home into a house with children, you must be certain

It is important to teach a child the proper way to pick up a Dachshund.

Did someone say "It's time to eat"?

Wire-haired Dachshund.

Smooth-coated Dachshund.

that the dog has been properly socialized to children. The best way to do this is to take your children with you to visit and interact with the pet at the seller's location. If the dog shows any degree of aggressiveness or shyness around your children, it would be best to look for another selection. One big advantage of purchasing a puppy less than 16 weeks of age is

Long-haired Dachshund.

Purchasing a puppy prior to 12 weeks of age gives you an opportune chance to form a strong, emotional bond with your pet.

Financial Responsibilities Associated with Dachshund Ownership

✔ Equipment and supplies (see Checklist, page 21)
✔ Books/magazines
✔ Preventive health care
  • Annual examinations
  • Vaccinations
  • Stool examinations
  • Routine teeth cleaning and dental care
  • Routine blood tests
  • Heartworm preventative
  • Flea and tick prevention
✔ Unexpected injuries or illnesses
✔ Pet insurance
✔ Kennel/boarding expenses
✔ Grooming fees (long-haired varieties)
✔ Licenses/permits
✔ Competitive events
  • Entry fees
  • Travel costs

that it affords you the opportunity to socialize it specifically to your children, but remember that negative socialization can also occur if a puppy is abused or mishandled in any way by a child, often resulting in aggressiveness toward that child when the puppy matures.

Your Dachshund and Existing Pets

Anticipate any jealousies or incompatibilities that a new Dachshund in the home would create. A most important consideration is how well your other pets have been socialized to

dogs and whether or not your new Dachshund itself has been socialized to other pets. If you have an existing pet at home that already attacks and/or runs from anything that moves on four legs, you could have a serious behavioral challenge on your hands when you bring a new dog home. Also, an unsocialized dog will often fight any new dog that trespasses into its territory. If you have pocket pets at home, including guinea pigs, rabbits, and ferrets, keep in mind what Dachshunds were originally bred for and make sure that all interactions between your Dachshund and these pets are always supervised.

Time and Money

With Dachshund ownership comes many responsibilities in terms of finances and time. Financial responsibilities include those costs associated with basic items such as food, dog bowls, and training devices, not to mention health care. Extracurricular activities such as competitive events and specialized training can also add to yearly expenditures.

If you travel a lot for your job or with your family, boarding expenses can accumulate rapidly, and you will need to plan on budgeting for such expenses as well.

Health: Be prepared to set money aside for your pet's medical insurance. Aside from routine checkups and immunizations, most Dachshunds will also need their teeth cleaned annually and have routine blood screens performed as part of their annual checkup. Certainly there may be unexpected illnesses or injuries that could catch you off guard financially and cause you to make decisions that you may not want to make but are forced to because of money. If you don't want to purchase an insurance policy for your pet—and many are available on the market today—consider self-insuring your Dachshund by setting up monthly contributions into a special "pet" fund.

Exercise and attention: As with any breed, idiosyncrasies do exist that you need to be aware of when considering the Dachshund as a pet. A big one for Dachshunds is that these dogs harbor loads of "compressed energy" and require lots of daily exercise and attention for proper relief. Dachshunds that aren't allowed to vent this energy become bored and frustrated, which in turn can lead to behavioral challenges and compulsive behavior, such as overeating and self-mutilation. Some Dachshunds that are left isolated for long periods of time, for instance, when their owners are away at work, can exhibit separation anxiety, an annoying behavioral problem (see Behavioral Challenges, page 49). If your work keeps you away from home for long periods of time, you may want to consider getting two Dachshunds instead of one so that they can keep each other company while you are gone.

Be sure to schedule quality time with your Dachshund every day, just as you would any other appointment or activity. This interaction can be in the form of exercise, play, or training. It should also include a few minutes of simply petting and talking to your pet. Daily brushing sessions will also benefit your dog, not only emotionally but physically as well. After all, who of us doesn't like to have his or her back scratched or rubbed on occasion? Take full

advantage of the greatest benefit of owning a dog: the human-companion animal bond. It has been proven that this bond harbors therapeutic health benefits for both parties.

Considering that it is not unusual for Dachshunds to live well over 15 years when properly cared for, the decision to bring a new dog into the home carries with it long-term responsibility. As a result, always think before you act and reflect upon these responsibilities prior to going shopping for a Dachshund.

Housing Considerations

If you are going to own a Dachshund, plan on making it a house dog. This rarely presents a challenge, owing to the Dachshund's small size, cleanliness, and trainability. Dachshunds that are housed outdoors away from the presence of their owners are prone to develop bad behaviors, including nuisance barking and digging. If you don't want a house dog, the Dachshund is not the right breed for you.

Your Dachshund should be provided with a special area or room in the home that it can claim as its own. If you are bringing an older dog into the house, ask the person from whom you purchased the dog where the dog slept when it was in his or her care and try to allow your dog access to the same location in your house.

For renters and apartment dwellers, the Dachshund is the ideal pet as far as size is concerned. Of course, be sure to check your lease closely for any pet restrictions that may be present.

FINDING THE DACHSHUND THAT IS RIGHT FOR YOU

Once you have satisfactorily answered the questions in the preceding chapter and are convinced that the Dachshund is the right dog for you, it's time to start your search. Begin by checking with your local breed associations, most of which can be found listed in telephone directories, Internet searches, or by contacting the American Kennel Club (see Information, page 100). These associations will be able to direct you to several reputable breeders, trainers, and/or pet retailers in your area who have Dachshunds for sale or adoption. Also check with other Dachshund owners in your neighborhood and ask where they got their pets—and any challenges that they may have experienced as a Dachshund owner.

Sources

Ads

Classified advertisements in newspapers and dog-related magazines are full of listings of Dachshunds for sale. Use these ads to determine what the going market price is for Dachshunds—both pet quality and show quality—in your area prior to going shopping. Pet-quality Dachshunds will cost less, as they may have disqualifying faults or defects that prevent

"Throw me the ball!"

them from placing in dog shows or field trials, yet these faults or defects rarely affect their quality as companion animals.

Puppy Mills/Backyard Breeders

Beware of purchasing your dog from puppy mills or puppy farms that mass-produce puppies, and from backyard breeders whose only motive for breeding their Dachshunds is profit. Chances are you'll end up paying too much for a dog that is of questionable genetic quality and has, or will have, serious health challenges.

Once you think you've found a reputable source, gather up as many references as you can of customers who have purchased puppies from the seller and call these references. If possible, go to the seller's location to observe and interact with the puppy or dog in its current environment.

Age of Puppy

The ideal age to purchase a puppy is between eight and sixteen weeks of age, as this is when socialization occurs. Obtaining a puppy that is older than sixteen weeks of age carries with it some risk if the pup has not been socialized or if negative socialization has occurred. As a general rule, select the puppy that is not too outgoing, yet not too shy—kind of "middle of the road." Puppies that shy away

Litter Size

It is best to select your puppy from a large litter of pups. If the seller is down to one or two puppies, there may be a reason that these particular puppies have not been picked; therefore, scrutinize your selection all the more closely.

from you can grow up to be fear biters and emotional wrecks. On the other hand, overly interactive puppies can be more difficult to train and tend to challenge pack hierarchy when they get older.

Before Purchase

Once you have a puppy in mind, fill out the Prepurchase Examination Checklist (see page 19).

If the pup passes this test, then plan on taking your prospective selection to a veterinarian of your choosing for a professional prepurchase examination. Reputable sellers will have no problem with this, but some may not be willing to pay for it. If you do have to pay for such a checkup, rest assured that it's money well spent. Any health challenges identified by your veterinarian and/or treatments needed should be handled by the seller prior to the purchase or else the cost of such care should be deducted from the purchase price. Also, have your veterinarian review the puppy's vaccination and deworming record to be sure it is current on everything. Often, new puppies that supposedly have had all of their shots and dewormings have actually missed a few, so be

sure to learn about this up front to prevent any unexpected financial surprises.

Trial Period

Prior to signing a purchase contract, request that a 30-day trial period be added to the contract so that you can assess your dog's personality and temperament in your home environment. This is especially important if you have children. Reputable sellers stand behind the quality and temperament of their dogs and will rarely have a challenge with such an arrangement. If the dog proves to be unsatisfactory for *any* reason, most sellers will allow you to return it for full refund—no questions asked! Nevertheless, be sure that this is stated clearly in the purchase contract.

AKC Registration

If your dog's parents are registered with the American Kennel Club, the seller should supply you with an AKC registration application that has been filled out with information about your Dachshund's physical characteristics, pedigree, and date of birth. The pedigree is nothing more than a listing of your dog's ancestry. To register your new pet, you must finish filling out the AKC registration application with your personal information and the name you would like your dog to be registered under, and mail the application, along with the application fee, to the American Kennel Club. The AKC will send you back an official registration certificate in a few weeks.

Competition

If you want to enter your Dachshund in the show or field trial circuit, closely examine the pedigree of the dog or puppy that you are

CHECKLIST

Prepurchase Examination

Evaluation of the Premises/Seller/Litter

- ☐ Clean and sanitary
- ☐ Adequate facilities for number of animals kept on premises
- ☐ Adequate shelter provided
- ☐ Seller handles puppies/dogs with gentleness and kindness
- ☐ Seller answers all questions freely and willingly
- ☐ Dam and sire appear healthy and well cared for
- ☐ All pups in litter appear active and healthy

Evaluation of Your Potential Selection

Attitude/General Appearance

- ☐ Alert
- ☐ Active
- ☐ Healthy appetite
- ☐ Playful and social
- ☐ Overbearing/aggressive
- ☐ Crying/uncomfortable
- ☐ Disinterested
- ☐ Lethargic
- ☐ Poor appetite
- ☐ Emaciated/bloated

Skin and Hair Coat

- ☐ Appears normal
- ☐ Dull, unkempt
- ☐ Dry
- ☐ Oily
- ☐ Itching
- ☐ Pustules
- ☐ Hair loss
- ☐ Scaly or scabby
- ☐ Abnormal lumps on or under the skin
- ☐ Parasites

Eyes

- ☐ Appear normal
- ☐ Clear discharge
- ☐ Mucus discharge
- ☐ Haziness/cloudiness
- ☐ Protruding third eyelids
- ☐ Redness
- ☐ Eyelid abnormalities
- ☐ Discoloration
- ☐ Squinting

Ears

- ☐ Appear normal
- ☐ Red; swollen
- ☐ Itchy
- ☐ Brown/black discharge
- ☐ Head shaking
- ☐ Hair loss on pinnae
- ☐ Bad odor
- ☐ Creamy, yellow discharge
- ☐ Tender
- ☐ Head tilt

Nose and Throat

- ☐ Appear normal
- ☐ Nasal discharge
- ☐ Enlarged lymph nodes (Feel on either side of the neck just under the jaw)
- ☐ Ulceration on nose
- ☐ Crusty nose

Mouth

- ☐ Appears normal
- ☐ Broken, discolored, or loose teeth
- ☐ Retained deciduous teeth (adults)
- ☐ Tartar accumulation
- ☐ Cleft palate
- ☐ Foul odor
- ☐ Tooth loss
- ☐ Inflamed gums
- ☐ Excess salivation
- ☐ Pale gums
- ☐ Ulcers
- ☐ Underbite/overbite

Miscellaneous

- ☐ Abdominal tenderness
- ☐ Breathing difficulties
- ☐ Loose stools
- ☐ Umbilical hernia
- ☐ Both testicles descended (male)
- ☐ Coughing
- ☐ Genital discharge
- ☐ Limb deformities
- ☐ Scooting rear end on floor

looking to purchase. AKC championship titles are indicated on the registry of the pedigree and are a good indication that you are purchasing a quality pup. Of course, such a Dachshund may come at a higher price, but if your competitive aspirations are high, this quality will help give you an edge over the competition. Talk to breeders in your area who have champion dogs and note what features, both physical and mental, that you should look for in yours. Attend dog shows and field trials, talking to the Dachshund owners in attendance. Many of these folks are breeders themselves and will be good sources for show-quality pets.

Unless you are planning to enter your Dachshund in AKC competitive events, there is really no need to purchase a Dachshund with AKC papers. AKC registration is no indication of quality and only increases the purchase price

Purchase puppies from reputable sources only:

of pets being sold. Of course, if you are purchasing your Dachshund from a highly reputable seller, the higher price may be justified. However, if you are purchasing a pet-quality—versus show-quality—Dachshund from a classified ad in your local newspaper or from a backyard breeder, or if you are planning to neuter your pet, there is really no need for such papers. In fact, reputable breeders will insist that pet-quality Dachshunds be neutered to prevent the future passage of the undesirable genetic traits that rendered it non-show quality in the first place.

For more information on selecting your Dachshund, see Inherited Diseases, page 76.

Before Picking Up Your Dachshund

Several days prior to picking up your new Dachshund puppy, take an old towel or blanket to the seller and request that it be placed with your pup's mother, brothers, and sisters. The fabric will naturally become imbued with scents that your pup will readily recognize. Such a towel or blanket can prove to be of great comfort to the nervous pup during its first few nights in its new home.

Other Pets

When picking up your new dog, you may want to bring any dogs and cats you have in your home along for the ride, if this is possible, so they can meet the newcomer on neutral ground as opposed to their home turf. This may help defuse some of the territorial tension that the newcomer will undoubtedly cause when first brought home.

Supplies and Safety Measures

Finally, plan on gathering up all of the supplies you will need for your new dog ahead of time, including its crate, travel carrier, or kennel. Also, when keeping any dog indoors, there are several safety measures to institute to protect your pet from accidental injury or poisoning.

1. Be sure to place all houseplants well out of reach. Many plants are poisonous or at least irritating to the gastrointestinal tract of dogs and could cause problems to inquisitive canines.

2. Cover or deny access to all electrical cords. Puppies love to chew on cords, and run the risk

Have a pre-purchase exam performed on your intended selection.

CHECKLIST

Equipment and Accessories for Your New Dachshund

- ✔ Crate/travel kennel
- ✔ Baby gate
- ✔ Food and water bowls
- ✔ Collar
- ✔ Name tag
- ✔ Leash (extendable)
- ✔ Brush and comb
- ✔ Toys (solid nylon or rubber)
- ✔ Food
- ✔ Nail trimmers
- ✔ Anti-chew spray
- ✔ Odor neutralizer
- ✔ Dental care accessories
- ✔ Heartworm preventive medications
- ✔ Flea control products

of electrocution if they bite down too hard on them. This may mean prohibiting access of your pet to certain areas of the house, but this is certainly a minor inconvenience compared to a potentially fatal accident.

3. Keep in mind that puppies will explore the environment with their mouths and will put anything inside their mouths, so pick up everything that is not a toy or chew bone off the ground, especially spare change. Make a concerted effort to keep these items picked up on a regular basis.

Obviously, you'll want to keep your Dachshund confined to non-carpeted areas of the house until it is properly house-trained, as even stain-resistant carpets will show repeated accidents over time. As a result, decide ahead of time which areas will be off limits to your new dog. Also, Dachshunds are accomplished explorers, so be sure to plug any holes, cracks, or crevices both inside and outside the house into which your new pet could crawl or burrow and not be able to get out.

Bringing Your New Dachshund Home

When you do finally bring your new dog or puppy home for the first time, you'll want to do everything in your power to ensure that his initial encounter with its new surroundings is pleasant and positive.

✔ If you have children, carefully supervise their initial interactions with your new pet. Be sure they understand that your new family member may be a bit fearful and apprehensive when he first arrives home.

✔ Allow your puppy ample time to explore his new environment and to satisfy his inherent curiosity. Introduce him to his own personal crate, carrier, or kennel and allow him some undisturbed time to become acquainted with it.

✔ Whenever you feel your young puppy is tiring or becoming exhausted from repeated bouts of playing and exploring, put him in his kennel and shut the door. By doing so, your pup will learn to associate the enclosure with rest and relaxation. Be sure that no one disturbs your puppy while he is resting in its new "den."

✔ If your puppy whines during his first few nights at home, resist the temptation to remove him from his enclosure. Most Dachshund pups will eventually resign themselves to their situation and stop protesting. Often, turning on a radio or a relaxing compact disc for an anxious pup to listen to will have a nice calming effect and distract your puppy from focusing on his perceived isolation.

✔ Keeping the temperature in your puppy's environment during the night between 76 and 80°F (24–27°C) will encourage a restful sleep.

The proper way to hold a Dachshund.

Naming Your New Dachshund

When purchasing an adult dog, it is best to keep the same name that was used by the previous owner. If for some reason you simply must change it, pick a new name that is similar in syllable length and pronunciation to the old name in order to avoid confusion.

Naming a new puppy should involve the entire family. There are many fun books on the market that can assist you in your selection. Choose a name with two syllables as this will help your Dachshund differentiate its name from the single syllable training commands that it will be required to learn.

Playing and Interacting with Your Dachshund

Stress to your children the importance of gentle play and handling. Be sure they (and you) know the proper way to pick up a Dachshund. Dachshunds should never be picked up solely by the front legs nor by the skin of the neck or back, as this can lead to injuries. Instead, you should pick up the entire body as one unit, keeping the dog's back straight and supported at all times and the hind legs supported against the body, not left dangling in midair.

As previously mentioned, because puppies love to explore their environment with their mouths, they will chew on everything in sight, including your hands and feet. When this happens, simply say "No" in a firm voice and divert your puppy's attention with a toy or chew bone. Avoid playing tug-of-war with your puppy as this can damage its teeth, and in some instances, can hurt its back. Do not use

old shoes, socks, or articles of clothing as toys for your puppy. After all, you can't expect it to know the difference between an old rag and a valuable article of clothing, so it is best to prevent such behavior right from the start.

Toys

Toys for your Dachshund should be made of solid rubber, nylon, or rawhide. Of the three, highly digestible nylon toys and chews are the most desirable, as they are least likely to cause gastrointestinal upset. Just be sure to check the label of the nylon product you ultimately select to verify that it is indeed highly digestible—not all nylon products are. Rawhide chews are fine as long as your Dachshund takes his time and chews slowly, as swallowing large pieces of rawhide can cause gastrointestinal problems. Also, some dogs may have difficulty differentiating rawhide from leather, which could certainly put your new pair of leather shoes in jeopardy. Rubber toys should be hard enough so they cannot be ripped apart

Puppies are naturally inquisitive and will put just about anything into their mouths!

extended vacation or a short trip to the local grocery store, there are some guidelines that you should follow to ensure a safe, pleasant experience for your pet.

too easily. And you should avoid any chew toys containing plastic squeaks, as these can be easily extracted and swallowed by nimble Dachshunds, resulting in an expensive trip to your veterinarian.

Traveling with Your Dachshund

As a rule, most Dachshunds are good travel companions; rarely do they become hysterical or sick to their stomachs when placed inside a moving object. However, whenever you plan on traveling with your Dachshund, whether on an

━ CHECKLIST ━

Puppy-proofing Your Home
Check off the following safety measures.
✔ Free access to stairways, ledges, balconies, and other elevations denied
✔ Access to narrow spaces next to refrigerator and other free-standing appliances denied
✔ Access to fireplace denied
✔ All houseplants out of reach
✔ No exposed electrical cords or sockets
✔ Toilet bowl cleaner removed from toilet
✔ Bookshelves, tables, lamps, and fixtures properly secured to prevent tipping
✔ All items smaller than a tennis ball picked up from the floor (coins, needles, tacks, toys, and so on)
✔ All household cleansers, chemicals, detergents, rodent control devices, and pesticides placed out of reach
✔ Garage hazards such as fertilizer, weed killers, oil, gasoline, and antifreeze placed out of reach
✔ Access to garbage cans or pantries denied
✔ Access to food other than dog food denied

Plan on paying more for the show-quality pet.

Traveling by Car

When traveling with your Dachshund by automobile, always keep the safety and comfort of both driver and passenger in mind. Dogs allowed to run freely in the front seat of a car pose a serious driving hazard. As a result, always use a travel carrier when transporting your Dachshund by car. Ideally, this carrier should be just big enough to allow your Dachshund to stand up and turn around comfortably.

Keep the interior of your car cool and well-ventilated. Dachshunds that are excited and forced to travel in hot stuffy cars or those filled with cigarette smoke can hyperventilate and overheat. Also, car exhaust fumes can quickly overcome a Dachshund left inside an idling car.

Be sure to puppy-proof your home to provide a safe environment for your newest family member.

If you get stuck in traffic, be sure to crack the windows and keep the air circulating within the car. And never leave a dog unattended in a parked car on a sunny day, or when outside temperatures exceed 72°F (22°C) or drop below 55°F (13°C). If you do, your dog could succumb to heatstroke or hypothermia, respectively.

If your car ride is going to last for more than an hour, be sure you take along plenty of water for your Dachshund to drink and plan on making frequent potty stops along the way. Ice makes an excellent, spill-free source of water for these long trips. If your Dachshund tends to get sick when traveling in a car, talk to your veterinarian. He or she can recommend several over-the-counter remedies that prevent carsickness in dogs, or, if needed, prescribe an even stronger medication.

Taking to the Skies

If you are planning to transport your Dachshund by plane, consult your veterinarian prior to your trip to determine whether or not your pet has any medical conditions that may prohibit such travel. For example, should significant tem-perature and/or pressure fluctuations occur during flight, they could be harmful to a Dachshund suffering from an underlying heart condition.

Since different companies may have different policies, check ahead of time with your airline concerning its travel rules and requirements for pets. Many airlines will allow you to take your Dachshund into the cabin with you; however, for your comfort and that of your fellow passengers, your Dachshund must be well behaved and quiet during the trip. If you fear that these two criteria will not be met, your Dachshund should travel cargo class.

If your dog is to travel cargo, book either an early evening or early morning flight during the summer months and midday flights during winter months to protect your dog from exposure to temperature extremes. Also, book direct flights only so that there's no chance of "lost baggage." If possible, plan on arriving at the gate early enough so that you can observe your pet being loaded onto the plane.

Carriers: If you own a pet carrier that is not fit for air travel, most airlines have carriers for rent; however, be sure that the pet carrier selected for your pet is the proper size for his safety during the flight. Call ahead of time to confirm carrier availability.

You will want to pad the inside of the carrier liberally with large blankets and/or towels. And don't forget to throw in one of your pet's favorite toys. A "Live Animal" sticker, as well as your name, address, and phone number, should be attached conspicuously to the outside of the carrier. Avoid feeding your pet within eight hours of the plane trip. Provide a constant source of water

When transporting your dog by air, be sure her carrier is sturdy and clearly identified.

during the flight by freezing water in a water bowl the night prior to your trip and placing this in your pet's carrier prior to the flight.

Vacation Planning

Prior to leaving on your vacation, there are certain items that need to be taken care of.

1. To begin, be sure you are aware of all the requirements necessary for taking your dog to his intended destination, including required health certificates, quarantines, and customs. When traveling domestically and interstate with your pet, two items you should always have with you are your pet's vaccination record and a current health certificate. A licensed veterinarian must issue this health certificate within ten days of your trip. If traveling overseas, the embassy of the country of destination can inform you of all of the necessary requirements for the safe and legal transport of your pet.

2. Be sure the carrier you have for your dog is sturdy and in good condition. Also, make sure your pet's collar has identification tags, including a phone number, if possible, of where you'll be staying just in case your pet gets lost.

3. Of course, you'll want to take a leash along for daily exercise, as well as your pet's brush and/or comb for daily grooming.

4. Plan on taking plenty of your dog's food along with you, just in case the brand you normally feed him is not available at your destination.

5. Consult travel guides or travel agents to find listing of those motels, hotels, and campgrounds that accept pets, and plan your overnight stops around these locations.

Note: Try not to leave your pet unattended in your motel or hotel room. If you do, be sure

to place the "Do Not Disturb" sign on the front door so that your pet doesn't accidentally escape if housekeeping comes to clean your room while you are away.

6. When you arrive at your destination, look in the local phone directory for the name and number a local veterinarian in the area, just in case of emergency.

Camping

When camping with your pet, don't allow him to roam or to interact with wild animals. Dachshunds, being the natural-bred hunters that they are, could get themselves in trouble very quickly. It's also a great idea to have your Dachshund checked out by your veterinarian following these camping trips to be sure he didn't pick up any unwanted parasites from the local fauna.

Leaving Your Dachshund Home

There will be times when your Dachshund will be better off at home than traveling with you. In these instances, choose a kennel facility for your dog as you would a hotel for yourself, making sure it is clean, well-ventilated, and staffed by caring people. Many newer facilities are equipped with interactive cameras attached to each run or pen that can be accessed over the Internet, allowing you to check in on your pet even if you happen to be on the other side of the world! Although it costs more to board a pet at such a facility, many owners feel it's well worth the price.

Another alternative is to keep your dog at home and hire a pet-sitter to check in on your pet throughout the day. If you can't find a neighbor or friend to oblige, check your phone book for a professional pet-sitter near you, or ask your veterinarian to refer you to one.

FEEDING YOUR DACHSHUND

A sound nutritional program will be a vital part of your Dachshund's preventive health care. It's a proven fact that good nutrition leads to stronger immune systems, higher energy levels, and healthier pets. Conversely, feeding a poor-quality, imbalanced diet can decrease longevity, decrease energy levels, create emotional disturbances, and increase the number of trips you have to make to your veterinarian.

Your goal as a responsible Dachshund owner is to find the ration that is most nutritionally complete and balanced for your dog's particular stage of life and activity level. Although some breeders and trainers advocate the use of homemade formulations, using meat and other natural ingredients as raw materials, it is not necessary to do so in order to achieve the highest nutritional plane. While homemade formulas can provide excellent nutrition, they can actually be harmful to a pet if they are not prepared properly and do not contain a proper balance of nutrients. Most pet food companies invest million of dollars in research and development to ensure that their products meet rigid quality standards. As a result, you should capitalize on such research and feed your dog one of these diets instead of a homemade ration.

Types of Food

Dry food: Commercial foods come in a variety of different presentations, including dry,

Unconditional love!

moist, and semimoist. Whenever possible, we recommend that you feed dry food to your Dachshund. Dry foods are by far the least costly and easiest to handle of the three. They are also the easiest to buy in bulk and have a longer shelf life once exposed to air. Transferring the contents of the bag into a plastic container with an air-tight, resealable lid can further preserve this shelf life.

Moist or semimoist food: Moist foods may come in handy when a dog is suffering from a condition of the mouth, teeth, or throat that may make consuming dry food painful or difficult. They also can be useful for feeding Dachshund puppies under the age of eight weeks that may have difficulty chewing hard kibbles.

If you do choose to feed moist or semimoist food to your Dachshund, be sure to discard any unused portion in her food bowl after every feeding. In addition, cover all open cans you place in the refrigerator to prevent spoilage. As a rule, any uneaten portion in a can should be discarded within 48 hours after the can is opened.

Bones

Just a quick word here about bones: With the vast number of bone substitutes available on the market today, there is no reason to feed your Dachshund real bones. Natural bones of any kind—especially poultry, pork, and any type of rib bone—can splinter and perforate or obstruct the mouth or digestive tract. Bones can also add unwanted minerals to the diet, creating nutritional imbalances. Nylon bones that are labeled "highly digestible" are good choices as bone substitutes and are available in various flavors and styles at your favorite pet store. Rawhide bones are also acceptable substitutes for natural bones, provided your Dachshund chews them slowly.

Feeding the Puppy

For Dachshunds, puppyhood encompasses the first 14 months of life. Keep in mind that these months will set the stage in terms of health and development for the remainder of your pet's years, so don't skimp on good nutrition during this crucial stage of life. Adolescent Dachshunds require diets that are higher in fat, protein, minerals, and energy to ensure proper growth and muscular skeletal development. Feeding a high-quality commercial puppy formula can help you achieve this goal. Shop for quality, not necessarily for price, when selecting food for your pup. Since there are so many brands to choose from, ask your veterinarian for his or her recommendation.

The question often arises: Are those high-priced dog foods really worth the extra cost and are they that much better than the other less-pricey varieties? To help answer this question, simply reflect on your own nutrition. Which is the healthier diet for you? One that consists of high-quality ingredients including fruits, vegetables, and whole grains, or one consisting primarily of fast food? You know the answer, and the same holds true for our pets. Feeding rations that are made from high-quality ingredients and highly digestible and utilizable ingredients offers much better nutritional value than feeding diets with more

questionable ingredients. Of course, as with our own diets, you can expect to pay more for quality, but in terms of health and longevity it's worth it.

Feeding high-quality food has another distinct advantage—less stool to pick up. Since most of the ingredients are digested and absorbed by the dog's body, there is less left over to adorn your yard. This is not true for lower-quality diets that may contain a lot of indigestible fillers that can certainly add to your clean-up efforts.

Changing Diets

Be careful not to switch from one diet to another in rapid succession in order to find one that your pet seems to like the best, as this can often lead to gastrointestinal upset. Instead, pick one and stick with it unless your puppy simply refuses to eat it. If you're feeding a high-quality diet to your puppy, vitamin and mineral supplementation will not be required. If a change in diet is necessary, do so gradually over a two-week period. Start by preparing a blend of both old and new diet consisting of 70 percent old and 30 percent new. Feed this for several days. Next, create a 50/50 blend of both foods, and again, feed for two to three days. Then, feed a 30/70 blend, consisting of 30 percent of old ration and 70 percent new ration. Finally, eliminate the old ration altogether. By easing into the new diet in this way, your puppy is less likely to experience digestive upset.

Amount to Feed

The amount of food you should give to your Dachshund puppy will depend on the manufacturer's recommendations, as well as on individual variations including breed, environment, amount of exercise, personality, and individual metabolic variations. Take the recommended daily feeding amounts and divide it into two feedings for your puppy—one in the morning and one in the evening. Put the food down each time for about 20 minutes, allowing your puppy to eat all she wants in that time period. Once the 20 minutes are up, pick up the food bowl until the next meal. Again, in the evening, put the food down for 20 minutes only. If your puppy doesn't seem to be finishing all of her food, cut back slightly on the amount you offer on the next feeding. Remember, all puppies, like people, are individuals, and will have unique metabolisms requiring varying amounts of nutritional intake. By feeding in this way instead of free choice, your puppy will quickly learn to eat on a schedule that suits both you and her.

Warning: Whatever you do, do *not* feed table scraps to your puppy. Not only will this create a nutritional imbalance, but it will also create a finicky eater and a beggar out of your pet.

Water

Always keep plenty of fresh water accessible at all times. Remember that Dachshund puppies travel low to the ground so be sure they can easily access their water bowls. For best results, consider offering filtered water for the same reasons that it is recommended for humans. Make sure to change the water supply daily and thoroughly clean out the water bowl at least once a week.

Feeding the Adult

At 14 months of age, switch your Dachshund over to an adult maintenance formula. The average adult Dachshund requires less fat, protein, and calories in its diet than it did when it was a puppy. It is best to stick to the same brand of food that you were feeding as a puppy to ensure that the transition is a smooth one. Avoid foods that claim to be complete and balanced nutritionally *for all stages of life*. These have been formulated to meet the needs of the most demanding life stage, growth. As a result, they contain excess levels of nutrients and calories unsuitable for the adult dog.

When to Feed

Most adult Dachshunds can be fed once a day. Again, follow the manufacturer's label recommendation concerning daily feeding amounts and then adjust accordingly based on your dog's individual needs and activity levels. For instance, highly active Dachshunds or those on the field trial circuit will require extra nutrition to fuel the energy expenditures needed for these activities. As a rule, active dogs require approximately 35 to 45 percent more calories than the sedentary dogs. Ideally, the amount of food you offer should simply maintain your Dachshund's desired weight. If you feed too much, obesity can result with all of its negative health ramifications. On the flip side, not feeding enough can lead to an unhappy, hungry Dachshund that whines, begs, and gets into the garbage, which in itself can lead to an expensive trip to your veterinarian.

Be sure to feed your Dachshund at the same time each day. Dogs are creatures of habit and are most content when schedules are kept. Avoid rigorous activity with your Dachshund for at least 45 minutes after a meal to prevent painful bloating.

Sound nutrition can increase your dog's longevity and improve his quality of life.

Weight Gain

If you notice your dog is gaining weight, cut back slightly on the ration you are feeding in order to reduce the daily caloric intake. If by doing so your dog acts as if she is hungry, add some fiber to her ration. Ask your veterinarian for good sources for this fiber. Adding bulk to the diet should help satisfy your pet's cravings without adding any extra calories.

Treats

Avoid giving treats to your Dachshund, as these are sources of unwanted calories. Keep in mind that feeding a 10-pound (5 kg) Dachshund

Don't feed your puppy table scraps, no matter how she looks at you!

Obesity is one of the most prevalent health challenges affecting Dachshunds today.

one french fry is equivalent to an average adult human eating an entire "supersized" order of fries. As a rule, dogs don't naturally crave particular food items; however, if offered "junk food," they can quickly develop sweet and salt cravings and subsequent finicky eating behavior.

Offering kibbles of your dog's regular ration at various times during the day is a great way to satisfy between-meal cravings. In addition, steamed vegetables cut into bite-size pieces make excellent low-calorie treats that are easily digestible. You'll be amazed how your Dachshund will love to munch on these.

Feeding the Senior Adult

Once your Dachshund reaches seven years of age, still another dietary adjustment is required

As Dachshunds mature, dietary adjustments are necessary.

to accommodate the aging changes occurring in her body and to reduce or eliminate clinical manifestations of disease. For instance, as a dog matures, its metabolism slows and its tendency for obesity increases. As a result, increasing the fiber content of the diet can help an older pet maintain its desired weight, as well as keep its aging bowels functioning normally. Decreases in sensory abilities, including those of taste and smell, may lead to a decreased appetite in older pets unless they are fed a highly palatable and aromatic food. Because old kidneys cannot conserve protein as well as young ones, a special level of high-quality protein in the diet is required to counteract such loss. Finally, special levels of vitamins, minerals, and essential fatty acids will also promote healthy skin and hair coat as the pet matures.

Older dogs can sometimes lose their appetite for a variety of reasons other than sensory loss. These can include, among other conditions, periodontal disease, kidney disease, and liver disease. If you do ever notice your older Dachshund decreasing its food intake, be sure to consult your veterinarian to be sure the loss of appetite isn't due to some underlying medical disorder.

Again, when choosing a senior formula for your dog, choose the same brand of food that you were feeding during the earlier stages of life. Offer recommended label amounts to your older dog, making minor adjustments as necessary.

For Dachshunds over 12 years of age, consider dividing their daily ration allowance into two feedings, just as you did when they were puppies. Smaller portions will allow their aging digestive system to better handle and digest the food.

As always, be sure that all bowls are kept easily accessible, as diminished eyesight and painful arthritic joints can sometimes make it difficult for an older Dachshund to reach or find the food or water bowl. Always keep plenty of fresh water available for an older pet. Older pets deprived of water can quickly dehydrate and suffer organ failure.

Dietary Management of Disease

Dachshunds suffering from chronic disease conditions or recovering from illnesses or injuries require dietary adjustments to help promote healing and/or to slow the progression of disease (see Diseases and Conditions in Dachshunds, page 73). Such adjustments can be achieved by feeding special prescription-type diets available from your veterinarian. For example, Dachshunds suffering from constipation, colitis, or diabetes will require an elevated fiber content in their diets. Also, dogs with pancreatic disorders often respond well to diets that are more easily digestible than standard maintenance diets. Finally, Dachshunds suffering from heart disease should be fed diets that are restricted in sodium.

Because nutrient balance is critical when feeding these special diets, be sure to follow your veterinarian's recommendations regarding amounts and frequency of feedings, and above all, offer *no* treats unless first approved by the veterinarian.

Occasionally, Dachshunds may be allergic to certain ingredients contained in a food. Usually, such food allergies will present themselves in the form of vomiting, diarrhea, chronic ear infections, and/or skin problems. If you suspect that your dog may be allergic to its food, ask your veterinarian for advice. Together you should be able to isolate the offending substance and then find the diet that does not contain the offensive ingredient.

Weight Control

Obesity is among the top health hazards that your Dachshund may have to face during her life; as a result, prevention of this disease is a *must*. Obesity has the same detrimental health effects in dogs that it does in humans. Obese Dachshunds are especially prone to intervertebral disk rupture and joint injuries. In addition, the extra workload placed on the heart can lead to premature aging of this organ, as well as other vital organs within the body.

Unfortunately, if your Dachshund is overweight, simply cutting back on her rations will probably not do the trick. Instead, a weight-control program that combines increased activity or exercise together with a reduction in calories is the way to go (sound familiar?). Special weight-reduction diets are available from veterinarians and should be followed for this purpose. Diets touted as *light* formulas or less active formulas are good for maintaining weight, but these are not truly formulated for weight loss. Of course, eliminating treats and other caloric sources outside of your dog's normal ration is vital to prevent the fat from returning.

How do you know if your Dachshund is overweight? For starters, study the breed standard (see page 7) and consult your veterinarian to determine the ideal weight of your particular type of Dachshund. Also, Dachshunds have distinct layers of fat located beneath the skin covering the rib cage and hips. If your Dachshund is carrying too much fat, you will not be able to readily feel the ribs or the bony structures of the hip when you rub your hands against them. Another place you can check for excess fat deposits is at the base of the tail. If a "roll" is observed here, your Dachshund is probably carrying excess baggage.

If your Dachshund is at her ideal weight, it is a good idea to routinely weigh her two to three times a month to ensure that this weight is maintained. Remember that a 1-pound (.45 kg) weight increase in a typical Dachshund can be equivalent to a 10-pound (4 kg) plus weight increase in a human being.

Controllable factors that can contribute to obesity include inadequate exercise, overfeeding, and feeding too many treats or table scraps. Although there is a widely held belief that neutering a Dachshund will cause it to become obese, there is no clinical research that really proves or disproves this theory. However, anecdotal evidence would indicate that neutered Dachshunds should be observed for such tendencies and appropriate management measures taken if they indeed begin to gain too much weight.

Certain medical conditions can also cause apparent weight gain in dogs. For example, hypothyroidism can lead to obesity in dogs so affected. As a result, any unexpected weight gain in your dog should be brought to the attention of your veterinarian.

TRAINING YOUR DACHSHUND

Training is a vital tool for enhancing the relationship you have with your Dachshund. Proper training allows you to establish your dominance in the relationship and prevents many behavioral problems from appearing in the future. It will also afford you the ability to safely exercise and play with your Dachshund, and enjoy other quality time outdoors. Finally, and most important in the eyes of many, proper training will help spare your furniture and carpet from organic adulteration!

Understanding Your Dachshund

Anyone who has ever owned Dachshunds knows firsthand that they possess an intelligence that makes them sometimes act almost human. They can also exhibit a tremendous amount of free will and stubbornness if they choose to do so. Knowing how to apply some dog psychology to our pets will help enhance the relationship we have with them and help us deal with behavioral problems that may sometimes arise. But before we can utilize such remedies, we must first have a basic understanding of the canine learning process that makes them act the way they do. Apart from inherent instinctive reactions, canine behavior

Proper training is the key to a healthy pet-owner relationship.

is influenced by two dominant factors: sensory perception and learning intelligence.

Sensory Perception

Sight: As you might expect, dogs perceive their world differently than we do. For instance, the visual acuity of the dog is about the same as that of a human's around dusk. Canines see general images rather than distinct features. If you've ever worn a new hat or sunglasses around your Dachshund, only to have it back away from you or bark in apprehension, it did so because it didn't recognize your new look.

Smell: By far the most important sense for a Dachshund is the sense of smell. The brain of the dog has almost ten times more area devoted to this sense than does the human brain. As a result, canine noses are so acute that it's nearly impossible to artificially mask a scent from them. Such a keen scent will obviously have a definite bearing on behavior in certain instances.

Hearing: The sense of hearing in the average dog is much more fine-tuned than that in a human, allowing it to detect much higher sound pitches at a wider range of frequencies. The upper range of canine hearing is thought to be around 47,000 cycles per second; almost 30,000 cycles per second higher than that for people. Even with its long, pendulous earflaps, the Dachshund has no problem detecting and reacting to a plethora of sounds that we can't even begin to hear.

Learning Intelligence

In addition to actions prompted by instincts and by sensory input, dog behavior is governed heavily by learning intelligence. The most basic type of learning exhibited by dogs is *habituation,* characterized by a diminishing response to a stimulus that is repeated over and over. This type of learning comes in quite handy when trying to manage separation anxiety in an anxious pet (see Behavioral Challenges, page 49).

Another type of learning in dogs called *associative learning,* where the dog creates mental links between two or more different types of actions, results, and/or stimuli. For instance, rewarding your dog for a job well done during a training session will create a mental link in its brain, where it associates the action with pleasure. The more often the specific action/reward cycle is repeated, the stronger the link becomes. Associative learning, as well as other more complex learning patterns, also influence socialization. By far the most important time in the life of your Dachshund puppy is between the ages of three and twelve weeks. During this socialization period, young Dachshunds link social acceptance or hostility to members of their own species, as well to other species. For example, if for some reason, a puppy fails to be properly introduced to other dogs, cats, or humans during this time, there is a good chance that he will not get along with them as an adult. The same holds true for those young puppies that experience some traumatic, negative event involving another animal or human. For example, if a male owner abuses a puppy during the social-ization period, it may grow up to have an intense aversion to all men. Also, if a Dachshund puppy does not have contact with children during peak socialization, it may not recognize them as "human" and fail to treat them with the same respect and friendliness as it does adults.

This socialization is so important that whenever you are purchasing a Dachshund older than 12 weeks of age, always question the seller about the puppy's socialization experiences and about the specific steps that he or she took to ensure that proper socialization indeed took place. If proper socialization did not take place, you may be faced with unexpected behavioral challenges in the future.

Basic Training Principles

To achieve fast and lasting results from your training efforts, you will need to use plenty of patience, consistency, and repetition. Young puppies, and even many adult Dachshunds, have very short attention spans. In addition, Dachshunds can seem stubborn and self-determined at times. As a result, expect training progress to be made incrementally over multiple, brief training sessions. For instance, four 15-minute sessions a day will yield more fruitful results than will two 30-minute training sessions. This will no doubt require plenty of patience and dedication on your part.

For best results, schedule training sessions immediately upon arriving home from work and prior to leaving for work. Your Dachshund will be excited to have you home from work and will link the training experience to his pleasure at being reunited with you. In addition, dogs are very receptive to learning after waking from a deep sleep. A good training session prior to leaving for work will give your dog a good dose of activity that may serve to reduce his anxiety upon your departure.

To give consistency to your efforts, hold your training sessions at the same time every day, and plan on giving your commands each time using the same voice tone, voice inflection pattern, and body language. Your dog will hear your words as sounds without verbal understanding, but he will soon learn to recognize those sounds, based upon the above criteria, and mentally link them to the corresponding action that resulted in a reward.

Repetition: Along with patience and consistency, repetition will help to ensure positive training outcomes. Repeating a command and subsequent action over and over will quickly create reinforcement in your dog's mind. In addition, for those veterans that have mastered their basic training, be sure to give training refresher courses at least twice yearly. In dogs, as in people, repetition is indeed the "mother of skill."

Rewards and praise: For quickest results when training, use food rewards and praise—both verbal and hands-on—for a job well done instead of physical punishment for a job done poorly. Make it easy for your dog to "win" so you can be sure there will be plenty of rewards doled out during the training session. Find a healthy treat—and there are many available commercially—that your dog absolutely adores and utilize it along with your praise for best results.

Dogs want to please their owners and will often go to great lengths to do so. As a result, when your Dachshund pleases you, be sure he knows it. Bear in mind that many mistakes are made out of confusion, misunderstanding, or lack of ability rather than out of disobedience.

TIP

Double Standards

Avoid double standards in your approach to training your dog, as these lead to the ultimate in canine confusion. For example, if you are going to allow your dog to sleep with you on your bed, don't get upset if you find hair on your sofa. Along the same lines, if you allow your Dachshund to jump up on you when you are wearing old jeans and a T-shirt, how can you reprimand him for jumping on you when you are in a business suit? In other words, set the standards of behavior for your dog and make him stick to them.

When a new baby tries to walk for the first time and falls, his parents don't scold him for doing so; instead, they encourage him to try again. This same principle should be used when training your Dachshund. He wants to please you; he just may not know how to do it right now so it's your job to show him how. Once you do, you'll soon have your dog consistently performing up to your expectations.

Negative Reinforcement

Certainly there will be select instances in which negative reinforcement is indicated; however, this should never take the form of physical punishment. Instead, an auditory reprimand will suffice. A sharp verbal "No" or loud noise from a can full of coins or an air horn—or any device that emits an unpleasant noise—can be used to quickly gain your pet's attention. Just keep in mind that if you are to use negative reinforcement, it should be done quickly, right after the undesirable act occurs. The more time that elapses between the act and the reprimand, the more confused and frustrated your dog will become. Any negative reinforcement you dish out should last no more than a few seconds. Also, avoid using your dog's name when punishing him. The last thing you want is for your dog to begin associating his name with his bad behavior or with the punishment. Finally, if you choose to negatively reinforce a behavior, always follow it with a command or drill that will lead to a positive response deserving of reward; in other words, always end your sessions on a high note.

Establishing Dominance

It is important to establish your dominance in your relationship with your Dachshund right from the start. There are three ways to do it while you are training, keeping in mind that the younger the dog is, the more likely he is to submit to your authority.

1. Maintaining control of your dog's neck region using a collar and leash is the first way

to assert your dominance. A dog is naturally protective of its neck region, since this is the first place an opponent will target during a fight. By gaining control of this area with the collar and leash, your dog will have no choice but to submit to your higher authority.

2. A second way to establish your dominance is to apply downward pressure along your dog's back region. In the wild, dogs assert their dominance over one another by mounting each other's back area. By applying pressure on your Dachshund's back with your hand when teaching it to sit or lie down, or by simply petting your dog along its neck and back regions, you are, in essence, asserting your dominance just as its wild peers do.

One word of caution: Because Dachshunds are predisposed to back disorders, only gentle pressure should be used when applied along the back.

3. Finally, by staying calm and relaxed during your training sessions, your dog will sense that you are in control. Dogs can readily sense nervousness and stress in their handlers and yours won't hesitate to take advantage of the situation if he thinks he can. Unfortunately, if he succeeds, reestablishing your rightful rank may be difficult. As a result, always carry with you an air of confidence and control whenever you are around your dog.

Types of Training

Your Dachshund's basic training consists of three types: House-training (see HOW-TO:

It is during the socialization period that a puppy learns to interact peacefully with members of other species.

*All Dachshunds should be trained to accept
a collar and leash.*

House-training, page 46), desensitization training, and obedience training. All three types can
be and should be started as early as eight
weeks of age. Anything that your dog learns
between the ages of eight and sixteen weeks
(called the "period of stable learning") will
become firmly entrenched in its mind for the
remainder of its life.

Desensitization Training

The first type of training your Dachshund
should receive is called *desensitization
training.* Unfortunately, this type of training is
often overlooked by most new dog owners, yet
it can be one of the most valuable tools for
preventing behavioral problems as their dog
matures. There are three categories of desensitization training

1. Contact desensitization

2. Separation desensitization

3. Noise desensitization

The first two categories should be started at
eight weeks of age, with the third commencing
at sixteen weeks of age.

Contact desensitization: The first type,
contact desensitization training, will condition
your Dachshund to allow its feet, ears, and
mouth to be handled. This is extremely
important for your pet's preventive health care
program, as this will allow you to trim your
pet's nails, clean his ears, and brush his teeth
without a fight. When interacting with your
puppy, make a special effort to gently toy with
and touch these regions with your fingers
several times a day. Don't attempt to actually
trim nails, brush teeth, or clean ears; instead,

simply go through the motions. Soon, your pup
won't think twice when you reach out and
grasp a paw or an earflap; just remember to
temporarily discontinue your efforts if a
struggle ensues. Any negative or painful
experience involving these areas during your
initial training efforts can produce the exact
opposite effect and create an individual that
will struggle vehemently when attempts are
made to perform these simple procedures.

Separation desensitization: The goal of
separation desensitization training is to
desensitize your puppy to being left alone by
himself (see Separation Anxiety, page 49). This
important exercise will help prevent one of the
most common behavioral disorders seen in
Dachshunds—separation anxiety. This type of
desensitization can be achieved by putting
your puppy in his travel kennel and leaving the
house for a predetermined period of time—
a few minutes at a time for the first day, then
gradually working up over several weeks to 20-
to 30-minute departures each day—being careful

not to make a fuss over your puppy or respond to his protests prior to leaving. In addition, when you reenter the house, wait several minutes before you let your puppy out of his kennel, doing your best to ignore his pleas. When you do finally let him out, immediately take him outside to eliminate. If you act as though your arrivals and departures are nothing special, your pup will soon get used to being left alone.

Noise desensitization: The third type of desensitization training to start at an early age is the desensitization to strange or loud noises. The easiest method for accomplishing this training is to regularly expose your puppy to recordings of various sounds, such as thunder, lightning, fireworks, and so on. Compact discs containing these sounds are available at most book and record stores, or can be tracked down through the Internet. Playing these recordings in the presence of your puppy for 15 minutes daily for three to six weeks will usually achieve the desired desensitization.

Obedience Training

In addition to house-training and desensitization training, obedience training should also be initiated around eight weeks of age. Obedience training involves the teaching of basic verbal commands that will allow you to control your Dachshund in any given setting. The seven essential obedience commands that all Dachshunds should know include *stop, stay, come, heel, sit, down,* and *kennel.* Rest assured that your Dachshund might object to your initial efforts; however, always remain firm and in control. If you give in to your Dachshund's stubbornness or self-determination just once, you're in for a long, hard road. Don't be fooled: Dachshunds are intelligent dogs and are easily capable

of learning basic obedience commands at an early age.

Collar and lead: Prior to training, your Dachshund must be taught to accept a collar and a lead. These two items should be selected based on functionality and not on appearance. Contrary to popular belief, a standard collar can be used for training in lieu of chain training collars, which, although effective when used properly, can be as equally as dangerous if used improperly. Just make sure the collar is snug enough so that your pet cannot slip out of it, yet loose enough that you can easily slip two fingers between the collar and the dog's skin. Plan on purchasing a 10-foot (3 cm) retractable lead for your dog. Not only will this come in handy for everyday use, but its adjustable length will prove useful for training purposes.

When you first put a collar on your dog, allow him to wear it around the house for several days so that he can become accustomed to it. Then, for two to three minutes several times a day, attach the lead to the collar and allow the dog to drag it around the house, supervised of course. After two or three days of this, your dog should become accustomed to having the lead attached to his collar.

After this initial "break-in" period, start leading your Dachshund around the house with his lead, remembering that his initial reaction will be to balk and to sit down when you apply forward pressure. If this happens, don't fight back and start dragging your dog along the ground, but rather, let up on the lead and wait for your pet to move voluntarily. When he does, apply a slight forward pressure with the lead, then reward him. Soon he will link the tug of the lead with a reward and will respond accordingly.

The Basic Commands

Stop and Stay

The command *stop* is probably the most important obedience command you're going to teach your Dachshund. It tells your dog to stop immediately and stand at attention when commanded, a response that could one day save his life if he decides to dash off toward a busy street or to challenge an aggressive neighborhood dog. Or, if your Dachshund is getting ready to take a giant leap off of a piece of furniture, the *stop* command could spare his back from a ruptured intervertebral disk.

Step one: To teach this command, and its related command *stay*, begin by getting your dog to walk on its lead. As he begins to walk ahead of you, say "*Stop*" and give a firm backward tug on the lead. If your dog stops, walk up to him and offer him a treat, and praise. If your Dachshund fails to stop on your initial command or if he begins to move as you approach him, repeat the verbal command followed by the sharp tug on his lead until he complies. Again, reward your pupil for responding positively.

Step two: Once you have your dog standing in place, command him to "*Stay*," while at the same time waving your hand downward in front of his face. Begin to walk away slowly, keeping the lead slack. If your dog begins to move with you, immediately command him to stop again and walk back to him, repeating the command if necessary, and rewarding for compliance.

Gradually increase the distance that you walk away from your dog with each training session until you have reached the outer limits of your lead.

Come

Step one: To teach the *come* command to your Dachshund, begin by first stopping him and having him stand in place. Now walk 10 feet (3 cm) away from the dog, manually extending the flexible lead as you go.

Step two: Next, turn and face your Dachshund, kneel down, and say "*Come*," followed by a quick tug on the lead. More than likely, your dog will rush into your arms on command. When he does, lavish praise and/or a treat is in order. If your dog is reluctant to come to you, repeat the process. If he still fails to comply, walk up to him, pick him up, and move him to the area in which you were kneeling, then offer a reward and repeat the exercise.

Just a note: Never use the *come* command to call your dog in for negative reinforcement. To do so will make your dog shy away from training.

Another effective method for teaching this command is to link it with one of your dog's most favorite times of the day—mealtime. By saying *come* as you put down the food bowl, you are sure to elicit the desired response. And because the food acts as a natural reward, it will work almost every time.

Heel

The *heel* command is used to teach your Dachshund to walk by your side.

Step one: To start, position yourself with your dog standing stationary on your left side and his neck even with your left leg. With the handle of the lead being held in your left hand, say "*Heel*," giving a quick forward tug on the lead as you do so, and begin to walk forward.

Much patience is needed to achieve desired training results.

Step two: As your dog follows you, continue using the lead pressure to keep him from getting out ahead of you, giving a sharp backward tug on the leash as you say "*Heel.*" Go 5 to 10 yards (4 to 9 m) at a time, and then stop your dog and reward for a job well done.

Step three: Repeat this process over and over until your dog catches on. If your dog does not move on your initial command, set up again and start over. If needed, give an encouraging push on the rear end to initiate forward movement following your *heel* command.

Interchange the *stop* command with the *heel* command frequently, rewarding your dog for correct responses. Once your Dachshund is comfortable walking in straight lines by your side, try taking him through some right and left turns, always keeping his shoulder aligned with your leg.

Sit

The commands *sit* and *down* are vital if you want your dog to compete in obedience trials or dog shows.

Step one: To teach your Dachshund to sit, have him first assume the *heel* position. Next, hold a food treat above and slightly behind his eyes, saying "*Sit*" as you do, and at the same time, pushing down on his rear end just above the tail. Once in the sitting position, offer the treat as a reward and give plenty of praise.

Step two: Have your dog maintain this sitting position for at least five seconds, then say

Avoid double standards when training your Dachshund.

Teaching the "sit" command.

When training, praise your Dachshund lavishly for a job well done.

"*Heel!*" and move him forward out of the sitting position. Again, reward for compliance. Gradually increase the amount of time you allow your dog to remain in the sitting position until you feel comfortable he has mastered the command.

Down

Step one: Teach your dog the *down* command by first having him assume the sitting position. Next, say "*Down*," while at the same time holding a food treat between your dog's front feet close to the ground and, if necessary, applying gentle downward pressure with your free hand between your dog's shoulder blades; note how this is different from the *sit* command, where the pressure is applied to the hind end.

Step two: Once your dog has assumed the *down* position, offer the treat along with lots of praise. Keep repeating this drill until your dog catches on.

Kennel

Step one: Teach your Dachshund the *kennel* command by first positioning him in the sitting position about 10 feet (3 m) away from his travel carrier.

Step two: Next, walk over to the carrier, open the gate, and with your hand tapping the entrance, give the command, "*Kennel.*" If your Dachshund doesn't move, use the *come* command, giving a forward tug on the lead. As your dog nears the kennel, tap the entrance again with your hand, say "*Kennel*," and direct him into it.

Step three: A food treat can come in handy here to coax your dog to enter. As he does, repeat the command, then close the door behind him and reward him.

Allow your Dachshund to remain in his kennel for at least two minutes before allowing him to leave it. Keep repeating the command and exercise until you achieve your desired results.

Plan on starting to house-train your puppy as early as eight weeks of age, since this is when your puppy's period of stable learning begins. Before beginning however, be sure your puppy is current on his vaccinations, since he will be going outside, and is free of intestinal parasites. The latter is very important, since the presence of worms in the intestinal tract will cause unpredictable urges to eliminate.

Outside Training

For best results, train your dog to eliminate outdoors instead of on paper. Often, owners can't understand why their new puppy has no problems eliminating on newspaper, but just can't get the knack of going outside when the newspapers aren't there. They seem to forget that, to a puppy, newspaper and grass are two different surfaces with different smells. To first paper-train a puppy, and then expect it to switch over to another type of surface is asking a lot. Also, puppies need to be taught right from the start that the home is not the place to go. By allowing them to eliminate on papers inside the house, you are sending them a conflicting message.

Elimination Times

Puppies have four fairly predictable elimination times—those periods right after they wake up, right after they eat, right after they exercise or play, and just before they retire at night. Make a concerted effort to take your puppy outside at these times, and, if possible, every three to four hours in between. When you suspect that your puppy has to eliminate—he may start sniffing the ground, circling, and/or look anxious—take him to a defined section of yard far away from the house. Not only will this make cleaning up easy, it may spare a shoe or prized shrub from an unexpected encounter with a "pile" or urine deposit in a high traffic area in your yard.

When the Puppy Eliminates

When your puppy eliminates, reward him, then take him back inside immediately. He will thus begin to associate the act of eliminating with the location. If a minute passes and your pup hasn't gone, take him back inside anyway. Don't leave him outside to play or roam. However, watch him closely when you bring him back inside the house, as he may suddenly change his mind and decide to go. If it looks like

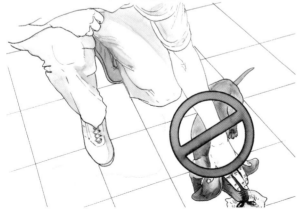

The incorrect way to housebreak a puppy!

Puppies will go into "sniffing" mode when they need to eliminate.

your pup is about to have an accident, immediately rush him back outside, and follow the same procedure as above. If you happen to catch your Dachshund in the act, simply pick him up and rush him outside. Sure, he may finish what he started before you get to the grass, but don't get upset. Place him down on the grass anyway, heap lots of praise on him, then pick him back up and bring him right back inside. Puppies trained in this way soon realize that their primary business for being outside is to eliminate, not to play.

Note: If an accident happens without your knowing it, don't get upset; that will serve no useful purpose. Simply try to be more attentive next time.

Praise

Always use lots of praise when house-training your puppy. Physical punishment will serve no purpose except to make your training more difficult, and to possibly desocialize your puppy at the same time. Whatever you do, don't stick your puppy's nose or face in the excrement in an attempt to prove a point. For some reason, this type of punishment is still quite popular among pet owners, even though it serves no useful purpose. In fact, if you really want to adversely affect your puppy's mental development, that is a good way to do it!

Feeding and Play Schedules

Establishing a regular feeding and play schedule for your new puppy will make your training easier. Feed no more than twice daily, and take your pup outside after he finishes each meal. It is preferable to feed the evening portion before 6:00 P.M. This will help reduce the number of overnight accidents that may otherwise occur.

Use an odor neutralizer on any region that has been soiled by your puppy.

Accidents

To help prevent accidents, keep your puppy in his crate or kennel, or at least in a confined area at night. This area should be puppy-proofed, and be floored in such a way that it won't be damaged if a slipup occurs. Utility rooms and half-bathrooms work well for this purpose. If an accident occurs during the night or while you are away, don't get upset; as your training sessions progress, you'll find that this will become less and less of a problem. A natural instinct of any canine is to keep its "den" clean. Such inherent instincts, combined with correct house-training efforts on your part, will help fuel the success of your training effort

Finally, if your puppy does have an accident, use a pet odor-neutralizing spray or cleaner instead of a deodorizer on the area in question. These are available at most pet stores, and will, in most cases, effectively eliminate any lingering scents that may lure your pet back to the same spot.

Nothing can be more frustrating to Dachshund owners than to experience behavioral challenges with their pets. Fortunately, by applying some of the information you learned about canine behavior and learning, most of these challenges can be corrected or at least controlled. In addition, by enlisting your veterinarian to play an active role in the management of the behavioral problem, the chances of success will be increased tremendously.

Separation Anxiety

If you have ever left your dog alone in your house, and she proceeded to chew up the furniture, bark or howl incessantly, and/or eliminate indiscriminately, you have seen separation anxiety in action. Because dogs are pack animals, they prefer to associate with others in their groups rather than hang out by themselves. As a result, your Dachshund will consider you part of her "pack" and long to be in your presence. Unfortunately, when you leave your dog alone, she may feel separated from her pack and become quite anxious. In cases of true separation anxiety, most of the destruction will occur in the first 30 minutes following departure.

Owners often unknowingly trigger an attack of separation anxiety by making a big fuss over their dogs when leaving or returning to their

Training should be started as early as eight weeks of age to help avoid behavioral challenges.

homes. Simple repeated actions such as rattling the car keys or turning off the television prior to leaving the house can also alert an insecure dog to an impending departure.

When addressing separation anxiety, remember that it is an instinctive behavior and not due to disobedience. For this reason, punishing your pet serves no purpose; in fact, most of these dogs would rather be punished than be left alone.

Treat separation anxiety by taking advantage of habituation learning in dogs (see Treating Separation Anxiety, page 50).

Nuisance Barking

Dogs may bark excessively for a number of reasons. The first is boredom; Dachshunds that are bored may bark simply to get attention. Another reason for constant barking is territoriality. Outsiders, whether they are human or animal, will almost always elicit a bark out of a dog if they are threatening to encroach upon her territory. Dogs may also use the bark indiscriminately as a message to outsiders to stay away. In such instances, the barking episode is often initiated by the bark of another dog in the neighborhood or by other activity in the neighborhood. Separation anxiety is another common source of nuisance barking. Some dogs will bark so incessantly upon their owners' departure that they develop laryngitis as a result.

In order to manage nuisance barking, avoid responding to your dog's barking behavior with verbal reprimands. Dogs that are barking out of

TIP

Treating Separation Anxiety

Here are some important points to remember when attempting to break your Dachshund of this annoying behavior.

1 Avoid any direct interaction with your dog for at least five minutes after your arrival to or before your departure from home. This will help keep the excitement and anxiety levels in your dog to a minimum.

2 Do your best to avoid reentering your home while the dog is performing the undesirable act. Doing so will only serve to positively reinforce the behavior.

3 Eliminate any behavior that may be tipping off your dog to your impending departure, such as rattling your car keys, saying good-bye to your dog, and other actions.

4 Try feeding your dog just prior to your departure. If the food bowl is put down as you're on the way out the door, your dog may link your leaving with something very pleasurable.

5 Consider leaving a television or radio on while you're gone to provide your dog with familiar sounds.

6 For refractory cases of separation anxiety, veterinarians can prescribe antianxiety medications to assist in the treatment of the behavioral disorder.

boredom or from separation anxiety will soon learn that their action will eventually get them attention—positive or negative. Regardless of which type, they'll keep barking!

It is important to rule out separation anxiety as the cause. If it is suspected, treat it just as you would any other case of this disorder. Dachshunds that bark for reasons other than separation anxiety should be given more attention throughout the day. A dog that tends to bark through the night should be given plenty of exercise in the evening to encourage a good night's sleep. Feeding her daily ration late in the evening may also promote contentment and sleep that comes from a full stomach. Also, try to encourage your neighbors to keep their pets indoors at night, since nighttime roaming activities of neighborhood dogs and cats are major causes of nuisance barking.

Inappropriate Elimination

Certainly one of the more annoying and disgusting of all problem behaviors in dogs is house soiling. This behavior can usually be linked to poor house-training as a puppy; however, it can also be brought on by separation anxiety, fear or submissiveness, excitement, territoriality, or, in some cases, disease. As a result, in order to eliminate or control the behavior, you must first identify its underlying cause.

Improper house-training: Improper house-training is by far the most common reason for house soiling. Just remember that it is never too late to begin the process. For older Dachshunds that weren't properly trained, train them as you would a puppy (see HOW-TO: House-training, page 46). Use lots of praise and reward treats to reinforce the desired behavior and speed results. During the training, confine your dog to her travel kennel if you have to leave the house for less than eight hours, since dogs are less likely to have premeditated accidents in such confined spaces. This will help prevent relapses, which can seriously undermine your training efforts.

Separation anxiety: Dogs suffering from separation anxiety commonly soil the house when an owner leaves. Some dogs will even go so far as to leave deposits on such objects as furniture, countertops, and bedding. As previously mentioned, behavior associated with separation anxiety will normally occur within 30 minutes of an owner's departure; such predictability can help you make a proper diagnosis. Treatment should proceed as with any other case of separation anxiety.

Fear and/or submissiveness: Fear and/or submissiveness often result in a cowering dog that urinates whenever anyone approaches. Dachshunds that received negative socialization as puppies are prime candidates for this type of behavior. Management of such behavior focuses on your actions and body language when approaching or greeting such a dog. For those dogs that urinate due to fear or submissiveness, avoid direct eye contact or physical contact when initially approaching them. Use a calm, soothing voice to help ease their anxiety. For the Dachshund that urinates when she gets excited, avoid making a fuss when reuniting with her after a period of separation. Instead, try ignoring her for a few minutes, or casually walk over to her food bowl and place some food or treats in it. The idea is to distract her attention away from the excitement of your arrival. Once you've been home awhile, then you can and should offer more of your attention.

Territoriality: Territorial instinct is another reason why a dog may choose to urinate, or sometimes defecate, indiscriminately, especially intact male Dachshunds. Dogs have such a keen sense of smell that the mere presence of a canine trespasser around the perimeter of the home, or the residual scent of a former occupant can cause them to start marking carpet, walls, and other objects in the home with urine. Neutering these pets at an early age may help solve this problem. A pet odor-neutralizing spray or cleaner should be used to eliminate scents on carpets, walls, baseboards, and furniture. Encouraging neighbors to prevent their dogs from roaming the neighborhood will also go a long way toward preventing this type of inappropriate elimination.

Diseases: Finally, certain diseases can cause a Dachshund to eliminate inappropriately. Internal parasites, urinary tract infections, kidney disease, Cushing's disease, and diabetes mellitus are just a few of the disorders that can lead to such behavior. As a result, don't just assume that your dog's soiling problem is purely a behavioral problem. Have the potential medical causes ruled out first, then you can concentrate on modifying your dog's behavior (see Diseases and Conditions in Dachshunds, page 73).

Digging

Remember that Dachshunds were originally bred to track down belligerent badgers, and often this required a great deal of digging on their part to complete their mission. As a result, you can be sure that a Dachshund knows how to dig! Fortunately, unless you have burrowing creatures inhabiting your backyard, most pet

Territorial instincts can lead to aggressive behavior.

Proper training and lots of daily attention can prevent most behavioral challenges from rearing their ugly heads.

Dachshunds will not exhibit this behavior to any great extent. For those that do, more than likely it is due to either boredom, hormones, or practicality. For example, if your Dachshund is bored, she may choose to excavate your yard just to pass the time. Similarly, a female in heat or an intact male that senses an opportunity with a member of the opposite sex will often attempt to dig under a fence to satisfy hormonal cravings. Still other Dachshunds, when left in the backyard on a hot day, will take it upon themselves to dig a hole in which to lie and stay cool. They may also dig holes in which to bury personal items such as bones or toys.

For the bored Dachshund, increasing the amount of daily exercise can help release energy that may otherwise be used for digging. Diverting the attention of a chronic digger is another plausible treatment approach; for instance, some troublesome cases have responded very well to the addition of a canine playmate. Rawhide bones and other chewing devices can also be used as attention-grabbers, but only if they don't end up underground themselves. If most of the digging occurs at night, overnight confinement to a travel kennel may be the only answer to your dilemma. If you suspect that hormones are influencing your dog's behavior, neutering is the prescription.

Destructive Chewing

Destructive chewing behavior often results from failure to properly obedience-train your dog, from an inappropriate selection of chewing substitutes, and from separation anxiety. Although puppies have a natural "pull" to explore their environment with their mouths, they need to be taught at an early age the difference between acceptable and unacceptable chewing behavior. For example, don't let a puppy play with and chew on old shoes or clothing. The puppy can't be expected to differentiate between an old shoe and a new shoe—they all taste the same! Instead, provide your dog with plenty of alternatives, such as nylon chew bones. Other moveable objects that seem attractive to your dog's teeth should obviously be placed as far out of reach as possible. For furniture or other immovable objects, anti-chew sprays—available in pet supply stores—can be applied around their perimeters to make a mischievous puppy think twice before chewing on them.

Note: For young to middle-aged Dachshunds, separation anxiety is probably the number one cause of destructive chewing. Solving your pet's anxiety will also solve the chewing problem.

Aggressiveness

Aggressiveness is certainly the most disturbing and the most unacceptable of all problem behaviors, especially if a dog exhibits aggressive behavior toward people. Dominance certainly plays an important role in canine aggression. Some dogs refuse to submit to authority and will lash out at anyone or anything that attempts to exert it. In many instances, these dogs were not properly socialized and/or trained when they were young. In others, sex hormones, namely testosterone, may exert a strong influence as well.

Treatment for aggressiveness consists of a return to basic command and obedience training. In addition, exercises designed to reestablish dominance can be recommended by your veterinarian. If the aggression is directed toward a particular person in general, that person also should be included in these exercises. Remember: Extreme caution and a good, strong muzzle are both advised before any attempts at such dominance assertion are made. For domineering male dogs, neutering is recommended prior to any attempts at retraining.

Fear and pain: Fear and pain are two common causes of aggressive showings in Dachshunds. If a dog feels threatened or overwhelmingly fearful, it naturally experiences a "fight or flight" syndrome and may choose the former option over the latter, depending on how it perceives its options. Obviously, you will want to remove the stimulus that is causing the fear reaction. If that stimulus happens to be you, you must exhibit extreme patience with these dogs. Be sure to allow them plenty of space, moving slowly around them, and talking soothingly to them. Often offering a tasty morsel to them will divert their attention away from their fear and help you to earn their trust.

Dachshunds suffering from arthritis or back pain may naturally lash out if picked up or touched in the wrong place. Other diseases can cause aggressive personality changes as well. If your once-docile dog develops an aggressive personality, your veterinarian should perform a complete checkup.

Vision or hearing problems: Older Dachshunds suffering from vision or hearing deficits may bite out of fear if startled. As a result, always attempt to capture the dog's attention using its remaining senses prior to approaching it.

Territorial aggressiveness: A Dachshund, like any dog, can exhibit territorial aggressiveness and opt to defend property that it deems its own, whether it's the backyard, the food bowl, or a favorite toy. A return to the basics of command training can help harness the territorial aggressiveness that may be exhibited by some dogs. Also, neutering dogs that exhibit territorial aggressiveness toward other dogs can sometimes help solve the problem. Certainly, showing some respect for your dog's "private property," such as toys, bowls, and other objects, and eating privacy is a common sense way to avoid this type of aggressive behavior as well. Be sure your children adhere to this rule too. If your dog seems particularly possessive over her objects, eliminate them altogether.

Prevention

The best treatment for most types of aggression is prevention. By adhering to the principles of proper socialization and proper command training, most behavioral problems related to aggressiveness can be avoided altogether. For tough cases, drug therapy can sometimes be used to make an aggressive dog more responsive to training. Consult your veterinarian for more details.

PREVENTIVE HEALTH CARE

A well-designed preventive health care plan will help ensure that your Dachshund lives a long and healthy life. Such a comprehensive plan should include the following:

✔ Physical examinations performed at home
✔ Immunizations
✔ Flea and tick control
✔ Heartworm prevention
✔ Intestinal parasite control
✔ Skin and coat care
✔ Ear care
✔ Dental care
✔ Exercise
✔ Neutering

In addition, sound nutrition and weight control are integral parts of your dog's preventive health care program. These subjects have been covered in a previous chapter.

The At-Home Physical Examination

Although cursory physical examinations performed at home are not meant to replace routine veterinary checkups, they are quite helpful for the early detection of disease and disorders that may germinate between visits to the veterinarian. As a result, you'll want to learn how to perform one on your pet. A great time to do this exam is during your dog's regular grooming sessions. The next time you visit your vet-

Preventive health care is the key to longevity for your pet.

erinarian, have him or her show you how to perform a cursory physical exam on your pet at home (see the checklist on page 60 that you can use to identify clinical signs of disease while administering the exam. If you check off Yes to any of these, contact your veterinarian).

Immunizations

Immunizations (vaccinations) are designed to prime your Dachshund's immune system to protect against a variety of infectious disease agents. Vaccinations against canine viral diseases are especially vital, since, as a rule, no specific treatments exist to directly combat these agents once they gain a foothold in the dog's body.

Most puppies will receive protective antibodies from their mother's colostrum—the special milk-like substance secreted by the mammary glands during the first 24 hours following parturition—if the female had received immunizations prior to pregnancy. These "passive" antibodies are important, since the immune system of a puppy less than six weeks of age is incapable of mounting an effective response to any disease organism. At eight weeks of age, levels of these antibodies begin to taper off, leaving the puppy's immune system to fend for itself.

For this reason, initial vaccinations should be administered at eight weeks of age. Vaccines administered to puppies younger than eight weeks are often rendered ineffective by the passive antibodies circulating in its system. However, vaccination as early as six weeks of age is indicated in those instances where the mother was not current on her vaccinations prior to pregnancy, or if lack of passive antibody absorption is a possibility, as in inadequate nursing during the first few hours of life. Unfortunately, at this age, a pup's immune system is immature, and may not respond effectively to the immunization. As a result, extra care should be taken with these puppies to prevent accidental exposure to disease agents.

Those diseases for which your Dachshund should be routinely vaccinated against include

Recommended Vaccination Schedule

Vaccine	Age of Initial Vaccination	Age for Second Puppy Vaccination	Age for Third Puppy Vaccination	Adult Vaccinations
Core Vaccines				
Distemper	8 weeks	12 weeks	16 weeks	Check with your veterinarian for recommended frequency
CAV-1 (Hepatitis)	8 weeks	12 weeks	16 weeks	Check with your veterinarian for recommended frequency
Parvovirus	8 weeks	12 weeks	16 weeks	Check with your veterinarian for recommended frequency
Parainfluenza	8 weeks	12 weeks	16 weeks	Check with your veterinarian for recommended frequency
Rabies	16 weeks	1 year and 4 months		Every one to three years (varies by state)
Optional Vaccines*				
Leptospirosis				
Bordetella (kennel cough)				
Coronavirus				
Lyme disease				

*Check with your veterinarian concerning the necessity of these vaccines in your area. Dogs that are regularly kenneled with other dogs should receive a *Bordetella* intranasal vaccine every six months.

✔ distemper
✔ parvovirus
✔ infectious canine hepatitis (CAV-1)
✔ parainfluenza
✔ rabies

Optional vaccines that are often administered to Dachshunds include leptospirosis, coronavirus, *Bordetella*, and Lyme disease.

Vaccination Schedule

For those Dachshunds over one year of age, check with your veterinarian for the ideal vaccination schedule for your particular pet. Many core vaccines may induce lifelong immunity; as a result, booster immunizations in adults that were properly vaccinated as puppies may not be necessary. See table on page 58 for more details.

Vaccine Reactions

As a breed, Dachshunds seem somewhat predisposed to allergic reactions to vaccines as compared to their peers. Although the overall incidence of such reactions is quite low, and the benefits of vaccinations far outweigh the risks associated with their administration, it is important for you to be able to recognize a reaction should one occur, and to respond properly.

Most commonly, vaccine reactions present as facial swelling and hives, along with itching and restlessness, usually occurring within 12 hours postvaccination. More serious vaccine reactions may be accompanied by profound weakness, malaise, and breathing difficulties.

If you suspect that your Dachshund may be having a reaction to its vaccinations, take the dog to your veterinarian immediately. He or she will be able to administer medications that will stop the reaction and prevent its further progression.

Dachshunds that have histories of vaccine reactions will require special vaccination protocols formulated by their veterinarians. Often, simply administering an antihistamine 30 minutes prior to immunizing will be sufficient to prevent any reactions; however, do so only upon your veterinarian's recommendation.

Intestinal Parasite Control

To keep your Dachshund free of intestinal parasites such as roundworms, hookworms, and whipworms, stool checks should be performed yearly by your veterinarian. Early detection and treatment of worm infestations will help prevent malnutrition, diarrhea, and stress-related immune suppression. It will also lessen the risk of zoonotic (pet-to-people) transmission of these parasites, especially to children.

Since the flea is a vector for dog tapeworms, good flea control is needed to protect your Dachshund against these worms (see Flea Control and Tick Control, pages 61–63). Disposing of fecal material deposited in your yard on a daily basis will also prevent any parasite eggs in the material from becoming infective.

Keeping your Dachshund on once-a-month heartworm preventive medication will also help protect against intestinal parasites (tapeworms excluded), depending upon the type you give. Check the label of the heartworm preventive medication you are using to see if it affords such protection against intestinal parasites. If not, consider asking your veterinarian to switch your dog over to one that does.

CHECKLIST

At-Home Physical Examination Checklist for Early Detection of Disease

Attitude, Posture, and Behavior

Yes* No

- ❑ ❑ Lethargic and inactive
- ❑ ❑ Abnormal posture
- ❑ ❑ Unexplained aggressiveness
- ❑ ❑ Increase or decrease in appetite
- ❑ ❑ Increase or decrease in urinations
- ❑ ❑ Increase or decrease in water consumption
- ❑ ❑ Scooting rear end on floor

Eyes

Yes* No

- ❑ ❑ Eye discharge
- ❑ ❑ Eye redness or squinting
- ❑ ❑ Unequal pupil size
- ❑ ❑ Cloudy or hazy eyes
- ❑ ❑ Eyelid abnormalities

Ears

Yes* No

- ❑ ❑ Red, swollen ears
- ❑ ❑ Ear odor or discharge
- ❑ ❑ Head tilt or shaking

Nose and Mouth

Yes* No

- ❑ ❑ Nasal discharge or ulceration
- ❑ ❑ Inflamed gums
- ❑ ❑ Excessive salivation
- ❑ ❑ Mouth ulcers or tumors

- ❑ ❑ Plaque and tartar accumulation on teeth
- ❑ ❑ Halitosis (bad breath)

Skin and Haircoat

Yes* No

- ❑ ❑ Excessively dry or oily skin
- ❑ ❑ Hair loss or excessive shedding
- ❑ ❑ Itching/redness
- ❑ ❑ Abnormal lumps or bumps on or beneath skin
- ❑ ❑ Pustules or crusts on skin

Bones and Joints

Yes* No

- ❑ ❑ Lameness
- ❑ ❑ Sore or sensitive anywhere along back
- ❑ ❑ Stiffness in morning or after exercise

Various

Yes* No

- ❑ ❑ Abdominal tenderness
- ❑ ❑ Vomiting or loose stools
- ❑ ❑ Coughing or breathing difficulties
- ❑ ❑ Genital discharge
- ❑ ❑ Mammary lumps

*If you answer Yes to any of the above, consult your veterinarian

A mass of heartworms removed from a single heart!

Heartworm Prevention

Dirofilaria immitis, the canine heartworm, is one of the most devastating and life-threatening enemies your Dachshund will face during its life. Transmitted by mosquitoes, heartworms pose a risk wherever and whenever mosquitoes are found. Imagine what it would feel like to have live worms moving around in your heart and blood vessels, and you will be able to empathize with the unfortunate victims of this disease. Heartworm disease places a tremendous strain on the heart, blood vessels, lungs, liver, and kidneys, adversely affecting the life span of your pet. Even Dachshunds kept indoors most of the time are at risk, since mosquitoes can easily gain entrance into a house.

Fortunately, administering a special medication on a monthly basis can prevent heartworm disease. Several types and brands are available; ask your veterinarian for a recommendation. In warmer climates where mosquitoes are present nearly all year, heartworm preventative will need to be given year-round, whereas in those regions that experience seasonal changes and cooler temperatures, preventative is required during the warmer "mosquito" months. Be sure to consult your veterinarian as to the proper preventative schedule to follow in your particular area.

If your dog is not currently on a heartworm prevention program, call right now and schedule an appointment with your veterinarian to

For your family's protection, it is important to keep your Dachshund parasite-free.

start him on one. A blood test will be required prior to starting your dog on preventative to be sure that your dog has not already been exposed to this parasite.

Flea Control

By far the most common external parasite that your Dachshund will experience is the flea. This parasite, whose bite can cause either localized irritation or a more generalized allergic

reaction, is also the carrier of the common dog tapeworm, *Dipylidium caninum*. As a result, diligent flea control should be given top priority! This includes treating not only your Dachshund, but also your home and yard as well.

Flea Control Products

When treating your dog, remember that dips and shampoos have little residual effect and are not especially useful for long-term flea control. Instead, plan on using one of the several new flea control products that have reached the market in recent years. Fipronil (Frontline, Rhone Merieux, Inc.) kills adult fleas on dogs and helps to break the flea lifecycle by also killing immature fleas before they can lay eggs. This product is also effective against ticks. Applied as a spray or topical solution, Fipronil collects within the hair follicles and sebaceous glands of the skin, providing good residual action after initial application. Imidacloprid (Advantage, Bayer Corporation) is another addition to the flea control arsenal that can be incorporated into a comprehensive flea control program. Imidacloprid works by killing adult fleas on contact, before they can lay eggs. Applied as topical drops on the back, Imidacloprid may be rendered ineffective by frequent bathing. Lufenuron (Program, Ciba-Geigy Corporation) is a product designed to be taken internally by your Dachshund. Available in tablet form, Lufenuron exerts its flea control action by sterilizing the fleas that bite the dog. Since they cannot reproduce, fleas are eventually eliminated—in a contained environment—through attrition. It is important to remember that Lufenuron does not actually kill fleas. As a result, products that kill adult fleas must be used in conjunction with this treatment in order to achieve effective flea control. As one might expect, many veterinarians rec-

ommend this product for those dogs kept in an indoor (contained) environment and that do not suffer from allergies to fleas.

Home Premises Treatment

Home premises treatment is best accomplished by sprinkling orthoboric acid powder on the carpets and near the baseboards of your home. Noticeable results are usually obtained within a week after application. Odorless, easy to use, and safe for pets and children, orthoboric acid is available under various brand names from your local pet supply house. Under normal conditions, application of this product must be performed every six to twelve months. Carpets must remain dry for continued efficacy; if the carpet becomes damp or is shampooed, reapplication will be necessary.

Finally, your yard should be treated with insecticide granules every six to eight weeks during the warm months of the year. Remember that fleas will proliferate in warm, dark, moist environments, so be sure to treat around hedges, under decks, and in some cases, under the house itself.

Tick Control

Measures used to control ticks on your Dachshund are similar to those used to control fleas. Fipronil (Frontline, Rhone Merieux, Inc.) is an excellent product that can be used to control both fleas and ticks. If your Dachshund frequents areas heavily infested with ticks, a flea and tick collar can help keep these parasites away from the face and ears. In addition, a pyrethrin spray can be applied to your dog's haircoat prior to a trip to the field to discourage ticks from attaching to it. If a few happen to slip by, use the same pyrethrin spray to kill those that have attached to the skin.

Female ticks will lay their eggs in and under sheltered areas in your yard, in wood stumps, rocks, and wall crevices. Once hatched, the larvae, called *seed ticks*, will crawl up onto grass stems or bushes and attach themselves to your dog if he happens to pass by. As a result, thorough and consistent treatment of the yard with an approved acaricide is needed to adequately control tick populations in your yard. Since ticks can live for months in their surrounding habitat without a blood meal, yard treatment should be performed every four weeks during the peak tick season in your area.

Grooming

Grooming is an important component of your dog's preventive health care program. Not only will such care keep your dog looking good, but it also provides a great chance to spend quality time with your pet. In addition, routine grooming will assist in the early detection of external parasites, tumors, infections, or any other changes or abnormalities caused by disease.

Brushing

You should plan to brush your Dachshund on a daily basis, regardless of the length of his haircoat. Brushing helps spread natural oils evenly across the skin and coat, encourages normal skin cell turnover, stimulates circulation to the skin, and rids the coat of shed hair. It also feels good to your dog and serves as a tremendous bonding tool between you and your pet. Initially brush your dog's coat against the lie of the hair, then brush it with the lie. Use smooth, long strokes when brushing.

TIP

Tick Removal

Never attempt to remove ticks from your dog by applying manual pressure alone, or by applying a hot match or needle to the tick's body. Most ticks first killed by the application of a pyrethrin spray will fall off with time. In some cases, you may need to manually remove the dead tick after spraying.

✔ When picking one off your dog, never use your bare hands in order to prevent your accidental exposure to diseases such as Lyme disease.

✔ Use a pair of gloves and tweezers to grasp the dead tick as close to its attachment site as possible, then pull straight up using constant tension until the tick is freed.

✔ Wash the bite wound with soap and water and then apply a first aid cream or ointment to prevent infection.

For smooth-haired Dachshunds, bristle brushes or wire pin brushes with rubber tips work well. A rubber curry comb can be used as well to provide an excellent massaging action. The coat can then be buffed with a chamois cloth to make it shine.

Wire-haired varieties can be brushed using a stiff-bristled or wire pin brush. They also need the long, coarse guard hairs hand-stripped from the coat after each shedding cycle, namely in the spring and fall. This is done by grasping the guard hairs at their roots with your thumb and forefinger and quickly pulling

Ticks can transmit a wide variety of infectious diseases to dogs, including Lyme disease.

Brushing your dog's teeth on a daily basis can help prevent heart disease when she gets older.

them out. Ask your groomer to demonstrate this technique for you.

Finally, for long-haired Dachshunds, a stiff-bristled or slicker brush can be used with good results. A comb should also be used after brushing. Be sure the feathering on the legs gets combed and trimmed as necessary. Excessive hair growing between the dog's toes should be trimmed short. Mats should be manually separated prior to their removal to protect the skin beneath. For added protection, place a comb against the skin at the base of the mat to further separate the skin from the scissors.

Bathing

As a rule, Dachshunds that are brushed on a daily basis rarely need to be bathed. Of course, if your dog rolls in dirt, grease, grime, or organic waste, a thorough cleaning is in order.

Plan on brushing your Dachshund on a daily basis.

Top: Routine cleaning will help keep your Dachshund's ears free from infection.

Right: Nail trims should be performed on a monthly basis.

In these instances, a mild, hypoallergenic shampoo formulated for dogs should be used. These shampoos are readily available from your veterinarian or favorite pet supply store. Also, if your Dachshund suffers from a skin condition, your veterinarian may prescribe bathing as part of the treatment regimen. Other than that, keep bathing to a minimum. Frequent bathing of a healthy coat and skin could cause irritation and dryness, predisposing the skin to disease.

Note: Prior to giving your Dachshund a bath, apply eye protection in the form of a sterile ophthalmic ointment available at any veterinary office. By doing so, you will protect the eyes from accidental soap burns and corneal ulcerations.

Clip back the toenails so that they are not touching the ground when the dog puts weight on the foot.

Nail Trimming

Examine your Dachshund's nails every four weeks and trim them if necessary. Nails that are too long will snag and tear easily, causing pain and discomfort. Also, nail overgrowth can stress the joints of the foot, leading to joint pain.

You will know your Dachshund's nails are too long if they touch the floor when your dog

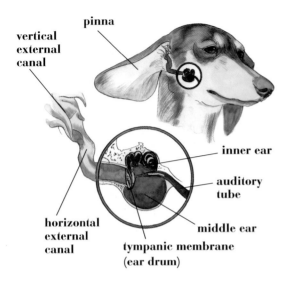

pinna

vertical
external
canal

inner ear

auditory
tube

horizontal
external
canal

middle ear

tympanic membrane
(ear drum)

The canine ear.

places weight on his paws. When trimming nails, use a brand of nail clipper that is designed for use only on dogs. If your dog's nails are clear, you should be able to note the line of demarcation between the pink quick—the portion of the nail that contains the blood supply—and the remaining portions of the nails. However, since the nails of most Dachshunds are dark, simply trim off small portions at a time until the nails are no longer bearing weight. If you cause a nail to bleed, don't worry—use a clean cloth or towel to apply direct pressure to the end of the bleeding nail for three to five minutes. In most cases, this will stop the bleeding. Ordinary flour or commercially available clotting powder can also be applied to the end of the nail to help stop the bleeding.

Ear Care

Because the ear canals of Dachshunds are long and the earflaps are pendulous, routine care for the ears is needed to prevent moisture, wax, and debris from accumulating, which can lead to infection. Your dog's ears should be cleaned every two weeks, using one of the many different types of ear cleansers and drying agents that are readily available from pet stores, pet supply houses, and veterinarians. Liquid ear cleansers are preferred over powders, since powders will saturate with moisture and accumulate in the ear canal. Most liquid ear cleansers contain ingredients that both dissolve earwax and dry the ear canal itself.

When you clean the ears, take note of any signs of irritation, discharges, or foul odors. If any of these signs are present, have your dog's ears examined by the veterinarian before you clean them. The eardrums may be diseased, and introducing a cleansing solution into such an ear can spread infection to the deeper portions of the ear.

Begin by gently pulling the earflap out and away from (perpendicular to) the head, a maneuver that will expose and straighten the ear canal.

✔ Carefully squeeze a liberal amount of ear cleaning solution into the ear and massage the ear canal for twenty seconds.

✔ Allow your dog to shake his head, then proceed to the opposite ear and follow the same procedure.

✔ Once both ears have been treated, use cotton balls or swabs to remove any wax or debris found on the inside folds of the earflap and the outer portions of the ear canal, but *never* stick these or anything else solid down into the ear canal itself.

Dental Care

As a breed, Dachshunds are fairly prone to tartar and plaque buildup on their teeth. In fact, over 70 percent of all Dachshunds will experience some degree of tooth and gum disease (periodontal disease) by the time they are three years old. If left unchecked, not only will periodontal disease cause foul breath and tooth loss, but can lead to an infection of the bloodstream that, in turn, can infect the heart and kidneys. Heart murmurs that arise in older Dachshunds can usually be traced back to a history of periodontal disease. As a result, regular visits by your dog to his veterinarian for professional teeth cleaning and polishing are a must. Professional cleaning should be performed every one to three years, depending on the rate of plaque buildup.

By instituting a regimen of daily at-home dental care, you can significantly increase the interval between professional treatments. Contrary to popular belief, feeding your dog hard chew biscuits does little to prevent periodontal disease. On the other hand, brushing your Dachshund's teeth on a daily basis will help combat this problem.

Toothpastes and cleansing solutions designed specifically for dogs are available from your veterinarian or local pet stores. Do not use human toothpastes, as these can upset your Dachshund's stomach. For best results, use preparations that contain chlorhexidine, an antimicrobial agent that can provide hours of residual protection against bacteria that may attempt to colonize the tooth and gum surfaces. A soft-bristled toothbrush or cloth should be used to gently massage the paste or solution onto the outer surfaces of the teeth and gums. If in doubt, ask your veterinarian to show you how to properly brush your pet's teeth.

Exercising Your Dachshund

Implementing a daily exercise program for your Dachshund is a proven way to improve his quality of life. Not only will it positively affect cardiovascular endurance, but it will also help tone and tighten the muscles and strengthen bones. In addition, agility and flexibility will be improved, which will help reduce the chances of joint and/or back injuries. Regular exercise also promotes gastrointestinal motility and stimulates nutrient absorption from the gut, ensuring maximum utilization of food. Finally, keeping your Dachshund fit will help to maintain his weight and prevent all of the health challenges that accompany obesity.

Prior to beginning an exercise program for your Dachshund, have your veterinarian perform a complete physical examination on your pet to be sure he is free of any health conditions that may affect the type and amount of exercise performed. Because Dachshunds have such short legs, they obviously don't make very good jogging partners; therefore, walking should be considered the exercise of choice. Considering that a Dachshund will take four to eight steps to your one, imagine the cardiovascular workout that is achieved by just 20 minutes of walking at a moderate pace!

Plan on exercising your Dachshund at least three times per week. Start out slowly for the first minute or two to allow your dog to warm up. In addition, at the end of the walking session, gradually back down the pace over a four-minute period to provide proper cooldown. Offer your athlete plenty of fresh water after cooling down to help replace fluids he may have lost during physical exercise.

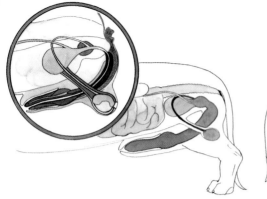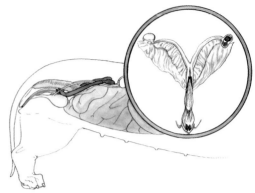
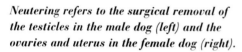

Neutering refers to the surgical removal of the testicles in the male dog (left) and the ovaries and uterus in the female dog (right).

For older Dachshunds or those individuals suffering from back problems, swimming is a great alternative to walking. Swim sessions lasting 15 to 20 minutes will provide cardiovascular and muscular health benefits similar to a walking program; however, just keep in mind that you cannot leave your Dachshund unattended in water. For safety purposes, consider purchasing a flotation vest for your dog

to wear while swimming; these are available through many pet supply companies, catalogs, and the Internet.

Neutering Your Dachshund

Neutering refers to the surgical removal of the ovaries and uterus (ovariohysterectomy; spay) in the female dog or the testicles (castra-

Dachshunds harbor immense energy stores and need to be exercised on a daily basis.

As your dog enters into his golden years, his nutritional and health care needs will change.

tion) in the male. If you are not planning to breed your Dachshund, or if your dog is older than six years, it is wise to neuter it. By doing so, uterine infections and pyometra in older females can be avoided, the incidence of prostate disorders in aging males can be greatly reduced, and the threat of testicular cancer eliminated completely. In addition, female Dachshunds that are spayed prior to their second heat cycle are also at a lesser risk of developing mammary cancer at a later age than are those spayed at a later age.

Contrary to popular belief, neutering your Dachshund won't make it lazy or fat—there

Schedule quality time with your dog each and every day.

Common Myths Concerning Neutering
- ✔ Causes laziness
- ✔ Prevents proper behavioral maturity
- ✔ Prevents proper physical maturity
- ✔ Alters a pet's personality
- ✔ Reduces pack protection instincts

are plenty of slim and trim neutered dogs running around debunking this myth. Improper feeding practices, lack of exercise, and, in some instances, disease, cause obesity in dogs, not neutering. Furthermore, while it is true that neutering can curb the desire to roam and interact with members of the opposite sex, your dog's overall energy level and behavior will not be adversely affected by the procedure.

Caring for Your Older Dachshund

Your Dachshund's golden years begin around eight years of age; however, your dog's chronological age may not be a true reflection of his physiological age. Genetics, nutrition, and environmental influences will all ultimately affect the aging process differently in each particular individual. Dachshunds that have received good nutrition and preventive health care during their youth and adulthood tend to live longer lives than those that don't receive such care.

The changes associated with aging are the result of years of wear and tear on the internal and external body systems. The table on this page lists the mental and physical changes you can expect as your Dachshund matures.

Management measures you should take to help your dog cope with advancing age include the following:

✔ Adjust your Dachshund's diet according to his specific health needs. For example, if your dog suffers from an age-related ailment such as heart disease or colitis, special diets may be prescribed to reduce the wear and tear on the affected organ systems. For the otherwise healthy seniors, feed a diet that is higher in fiber and reduced in calories to prevent obesity.

✔ Weigh your older dog on a monthly basis. Persistent weight loss or weight gain should be reported to your veterinarian.

✔ Maintain a moderate exercise program for your older dog to help keep his bones, joints, heart, and lungs conditioned. Consult your veterinarian first about the type and amount of exercise appropriate for your older pet.

✔ Brush your dog daily. Skin and coat changes secondary to aging, such as oily skin and abnormal shedding, can often be managed well with proper grooming. In addition, keep the toenails trimmed short. Older Dachshunds suffering from arthritis don't need the added challenge and pain of having to ambulate with nails growing to the floor.

✔ Semiannual veterinary checkups, routine teeth cleaning, and periodic at-home checkovers for aging pets are a must. Remember: Early detection of a disease condition is the key to curing or managing the disorder. Also,

Physical and Mental Changes Associated with Aging

Overall Metabolism	Reduced ability to regulate body temperature, reduction in metabolic rate leading to predisposition to obesity and decreased physical activity
Cardiovascular System	Reduced pumping efficiency of the heart, loss of blood vessel elasticity, increased blood pressure
Reproductive System	Enlargement of prostate gland (intact males), increased susceptibility to uterine infections (intact females), increased susceptibility to mammary tumors
Urinary System	Reduced kidney function, loss of bladder sphincter tone, leading to incontinence
Digestive System	Periodontal disease, tooth loss, mouth ulcers, overgrowth of gums, decreased liver and pancreatic function, altered intestinal digestion and absorption capabilities, reduced tolerance to dietary fluctuations and excesses, reduced colon motility
Endocrine System	Reduced hormone production, increased susceptibility to glandular tumors
Skin and Coat	Loss of skin elasticity, increase in skin thickness, thinning of haircoat, brittle toenails, increased susceptibility to skin tumors, altered sebaceous gland activity, graying of muzzle
Musculoskeletal System	Loss of muscle mass and tone, reduced bone pliability and joint mobility, arthritis and degenerative joint disease
Nervous System	Reduced reaction time to stimuli, diminished memory (senility), reduction in overall sensory acuity (all five senses); finicky appetite, sclerosis of eye lenses/cataracts
Immune System	Decreased immune competence, increased susceptibility to cancer, infectious diseases, and allergies

because of the effects aging has on the immune system, be sure to keep your dog current on his vaccinations.

✔ Be considerate of your older dog's limitations, both mentally and physically. Keep food and water bowls easily accessible. Provide ramps where necessary to help an arthritic dog negotiate steps and heights. To compensate for decreased sensory awareness, approach older dogs slower than you would younger ones, using a calm, reassuring voice to further enhance recognition.

✔ Be sure to give your old friend plenty of quality attention every day, continually reinforcing the companionship and bond that you two share together.

DISEASES AND CONDITIONS IN DACHSHUNDS

As a general rule, the Dachshund breed is a hearty and vigorous one. However, remember that dogs are similar to people in that some will go through their entire lives the picture of health, while others seem to spend more time at the veterinary (doctor's) office than they do at home!

Dachshunds are not unique in their predisposition and susceptibility to common canine diseases and disorders. As a result, it is beyond the scope of this book to provide a comprehensive review of *all* of the potential health challenges that your Dachshund may face, but there are numerous excellent books on the market today that focus specifically on diseases and disorders in dogs. Ask your veterinarian to recommend one.

Talking with Your Veterinarian

Whenever talking with your veterinarian concerning a health matter involving your Dachshund, you should never feel intimidated, rushed, or overwhelmed by the information given to you. The welfare of your pet depends on your ability to assess his health data and understand its ramifications. As a result, never hesitate to ask questions and keep asking until

As a rule, the Dachshund breed is quite hearty and vigorous.

you feel comfortable with the answers you are getting. Use the following checklist to help guide your line of questioning.

Note: Always ask for a written estimate of charges, as this will usually reveal your veterinarian's diagnostic and treatment plan for your pet in a nutshell. And if you'd like a second opinion, ask your veterinarian for names and phone numbers of veterinary specialists. Most veterinarians will not hesitate to set up a referral upon client request.

Laboratory Tests
✔ What is the purpose of this test? Why is it needed?
✔ How accurate is the test? Can there be false readings?
✔ Are there risks or side effects associated with performing the test?
✔ How much does the test cost?
✔ What is the logical sequence of testing that should be followed in order to achieve a diagnosis?

Diagnosis
✔ Which physical exam or laboratory findings led to this diagnosis?
✔ Is this a confirmed diagnosis or a differential diagnosis (one of many possibilities)?

Prognosis
✔ What is the prognosis with treatment? Without treatment?

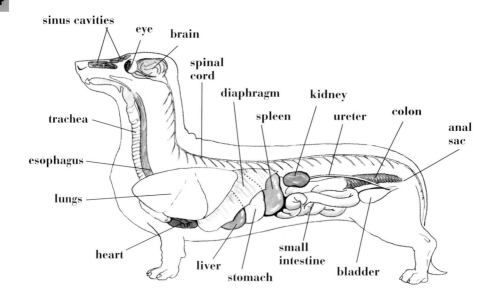

The internal organs of the Dachshund.

✔ Is the condition curable, or only manageable?
✔ How will my pet's overall quality of life be affected?

Treatment Plan
✔ Why does my pet need this particular treatment or medications?
✔ Is there a less expensive, yet effective alternative?
✔ What are the potential side effects, if any, to the treatment?
✔ What do I do if side effects occur?
✔ How soon should I see improvement?

Medications
✔ Do the medications need to be stored in a special way?
✔ Should the medication be given with a meal or between meals?

Costs
✔ May I please have a written estimate?

✔ Do you extend terms or is payment required at the time services are rendered?
✔ Do you recommend a pet health insurance plan?

Diseases and Disorders
All diseases and disorders can be classified into eight categories, depending on the underlying etiology. Understand that there can be a variety of overlaps between these categories, with one predisposing to the formation of another, or with two or more categories coexisting.

Inherited Diseases
Inherited diseases are passed from parents to puppies via the parents' chromosomes and genes. Many are congenital in nature; that is,

Recognized Genetic Diseases in Dachshunds

Disease Name	Clinical Presentation

Eyes and Ears

Chorioretinal dysplasia	Vision deficits
Heterochromia iridis	Different-colored irises; not known to cause vision deficits
Microphthalmia	Small eyeballs; may be associated with reduced vision
Congenital cataracts	Opaque eye lenses; blindness
Entropion	Inverted lower eyelids causing eye irritation
Glaucoma	Increase pressure within eye; blindness
Progressive retinal atrophy (PRA)	Progressive loss of vision
Keratoconjunctivitis sicca (KCS)	Reduced tear production, leading to eye irritation
Nerve deafness	Deafness

Skin and Soft Tissue

Demodectic mange	Skin parasite leading to hair loss and skin infections
Pemphigus	Autoimmune disease causing skin ulcerations and infections
Panniculitis	Painful inflammation of fat located beneath the skin
Pattern baldness	Hair loss that begins prior to one year of age
Alopecia	Lack or thinning of hair on earflaps, belly

Bones and Joints

Intervertebral disc disease	Pain, partial or full paralysis of hind limbs
Achondroplasia	Abnormal shortening of long bones
Osteopetrosis	Splayed legs; "swimmer" pups
Ununited anconeal process	Lameness

Mouth

Cleft palate	Opening in hard palate leading to aspiration pheumonia
Prognatia	Projecting upper jaw

Nervous System

Epilepsy	Seizures

Urinary System

Renal hypoplasia	Underdeveloped kidneys; increased thirst and urination
Uroliths	Bladder stones, leading to irritation, infection, or obstruction

Other

Diabetes mellitus	Weight loss, cataracts
Hypothyroidism	Weight gain, chronic infections, lethargy
Cushing's disease	Pot-bellied appearance; increased urinations; skin infections

they are present at birth. Others may not become apparent until a dog is several months old. Genetic defects are not especially common in Dachshunds, but when they do rear their ugly head, they can be quite devastating in their effect to the dog and to a breeding program.

Cutaneous asthenia is the name given to a group of devastating heredity diseases that have been known to occur in the Dachshund breed on rare occasion. Characterized by extreme skin fragility, puppies so affected develop large tears in the skin at even the slightest trauma. Blindness is also a feature of this condition. Unfortunately, there is no effective treatment or management for this disease, with secondary infections often claiming the lives of many of these dogs.

von Willebrand's disease is characterized by a defect in the body's ability to form blood clots in the event of internal or external bleeding. In affected Dachshunds, uncontrolled hemorrhages in and around organs, joints, muscles, and body cavities can occur secondary to even the most minor trauma to the body. Large swellings involving joints, abdomen, and tissues beneath the skin lead to marked lameness and soreness in these dogs. If bleeding occurs in the chest cavity, breathing difficulties arise as well. Cuts and punctures through the skin also result in bleeding that is difficult to control. Finally, Dachshunds afflicted with von Willebrand's disease are often weak and lethargic due to the secondary anemia resulting from internal bleeding.

The diagnosis of this disorder can be made in the laboratory; treatment of acute episodes involves transfusions of fresh blood or blood plasma. Although some bleeding episodes can be life threatening, most can be controlled through prompt veterinary intervention.

Cryptorchidism (retained, undescended testicles) is another less serious genetic defect that is sometimes seen in Dachshund puppies. Dachshunds with one or more retained testicles should be neutered as soon as possible. Testicles that are retained in the body can develop cancer over time if not removed.

Neutering known defective or carrier animals controls the spread of genetically based diseases. Such dogs may be sometimes difficult to identify if the defect is not outwardly noticeable.

When buying a Dachshund, there are a number of steps or precautions you should take to reduce the chances of unknowingly purchasing a dog with a genetic defect or one harboring a defective gene.

1. Only deal with reputable sellers when selecting your Dachshund.

2. Always ask for references of owners who have purchased puppies originating from the breeding pair your puppy will come from, and call them all.

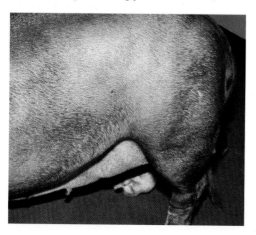

Hair thinning caused by hypothyroidism.

Obese Dachshunds are highly susceptible to disk disease.

3. Always examine your puppy's pedigree prior to purchase.

4. Discuss any questions you may have with the seller and be sure you feel comfortable with the answers you get.

5. Be sure to give your puppy a thorough check-over in its own environment, and insist on a physical exam by a veterinarian of your choice.

Metabolic Diseases

Metabolic diseases are caused by organ malfunctions in the body, resulting in abnormalities in hormone production and/or metabolic processes. Metabolic diseases can manifest themselves outwardly with a wide variety of clinical signs, and can be easily overlooked as the underlying cause of the symptoms. In fact, many metabolic diseases cannot be detected by a physical exam alone; a thorough laboratory workup is required in most cases to confirm or rule out these conditions.

Hypothyroidism is a metabolic disease that can appear in Dachshunds. Thyroid hormone is produced by the thyroid gland located near the base of the neck. This hormone functions to enhance the utilization of nutrients and oxygen in the body, thereby driving metabolism. If there is a deficiency in this hormone, the dog is said to have hypothyroidism. The causes of hypothyroidism can include immune system disorders, iodine deficiencies, and malfunctions of the pituitary gland. Clinical signs include lethargy, exercise intolerance, and intolerance to environmental temperature fluctuations. Affected Dachshunds tend to gain weight despite poor appetites. Dogs suffering from hypothyroidism will exhibit skin and haircoat changes as well. A generalized thinning of the coat takes place, the skin thickens and tends to droop, and seborrhea is usually present. Advanced cases of hypothyroidism can also lead to vision loss, nerve disorders, and joint inflammation is not treated properly.

Hypothyroidism can be easily diagnosed using simple blood-testing procedures. If diagnosed, treatment of this disorder entails the administration of synthetic thyroid hormone in liquid or tablet form on a daily basis, usually for the remainder of the dog's life.

Cushing's disease is another metabolic disease affecting Dachshunds. This condition is characterized by a chronic overproduction of steroid hormones in the dog's body, leading to those clinical signs typified by such an overdose. The most common cause of this disease is a tumor affecting specific glands in the dog's body. Seen most often in Dachshunds over eight years old, the condition causes profound increases in thirst and appetite, an increase in elimination activity, lethargy and exercise intolerance, and a generalized reduction in muscle size and tone, which leads to a characteristic potbellied appearance. Hair loss and skin infections are common in these dogs, as are eye ulcers. Because high levels of steroids will suppress the body's immune system, other infections, including those involving the bladder, can appear as well. Finally, if a tumor is the cause of the disease, the dog may suffer from seizures as the tumor grows and puts pressure on the brain.

Clinical signs, along with special blood tests, can be used to diagnose Cushing's disease. Special medications designed to control the production of steroid hormones in the body can be prescribed once a diagnosis is confirmed.

Therapy is usually required for life. Surgical removal of the tumor in the affected endocrine gland can also be attempted in severe cases, but this is a very difficult procedure that has many postoperative complications.

Immune-mediated Diseases

It seems ironic that some diseases are caused by the same body system designed to protect against disease, but immune-mediated diseases are not at all uncommon in dogs. Allergies are types of immune-mediated diseases in which the body overreacts to the presence of a foreign substance and causes an "allergic reaction" (see Allergic Reactions, page 87). More severe autoimmune diseases, such as pemphigus, can actually cause tissue damage and organ failure if not brought under medical control promptly.

Inhalant allergies can be initiated by breathing air containing grass and tree pollens, molds, dander, house dust, and hair. Signs of this type of allergy include face rubbing, licking and chewing at the feet, scratching behind the elbows and shoulders, and symmetrical hair loss. Small red bumps may be noticeable on the skin of affected dogs, and secondary skin infections due to the biting and scratching can occur as well. Because the ear canals of allergic dogs often become inflamed, ear infections can result.

The diagnosis of inhalant allergies is made using clinical signs, such as seasonal versus nonseasonal, response to treatment, and/or allergy testing. The latter may involve actual injections of potential allergy-causing agents into the skin and observing for reactions (intradermal testing) or less reliably, evaluation of blood serum samples for antibodies to offending agents. Traditionally, steroid antiinflammatory drugs have proven most useful in the control of the clinical signs associated with inhalant allergies. However, because long-term continuous use can cause deleterious side effects, one or more of the other modes of treatment should be considered. Oral administration of antihistamine medications, combined with omega-3 fatty acid therapy and daily oatmeal conditioning sprays, followed by brushing, can provide a satisfactory substitute for steroid therapy for many Dachshunds. For others, hyposensitization injections containing extracts of the substance(s) causing the allergy, identified by intradermal testing, can be successfully given to condition the body to ignore the presence of the offending substance.

Flea allergy: Apart from the itching and irritation caused by the mechanical action of fleas biting the skin, the itching and hair loss seen with a flea allergy are the result of an allergic response by the body to flea saliva deposited into the skin. The clinical signs of a flea allergy tend to localize along the back, especially near the base of the tail, hips, and rear legs. Diagnosis is determined by the presence of fleas on the dog, and upon distribution of clinical signs. Obviously, flea control is the treatment of choice for this disorder. In addition, the same type of treatments used to control inhalant allergies can be used to help reduce clinical signs associated with flea allergies.

Infectious/Parasitic Diseases

Infectious diseases in Dachshunds can be caused by a multitude of viral, bacterial, and fungal organisms found in nature. Dogs allowed to roam and interact indiscriminately with other animals and those that have not been properly vaccinated are at greatest risk of contracting an infectious disease. Intestinal parasites are also very common in dogs, and apart from causing gastrointestinal upset, can cause skin disorders, malnutrition, and immune system suppression. External parasites, such as fleas, ticks, and mange mites, can carry with them their share of health problems as well.

Viruses:

Canine Distemper. This infamous viral disease of dogs used to be one of the leading causes of death in unvaccinated puppies throughout the world. Although the incidence of this disease has decreased dramatically over the years due to vaccination programs, the distemper virus is still out there and can strike without warning. Infected dogs shed the disease in all body excretions, and transmission usually occurs via airborne means. As a result, as with canine cough, it is highly contagious and can travel some distance on an air current. Distemper is considered a multifaceted disease; that is, it can affect a number of different body systems, including the respiratory, gastrointestinal, and nervous systems. Coughing, breathing difficulties, eye and nose discharges, vomiting and diarrhea, blindness, paralysis, and seizures are just some of the clinical signs that can result from infection. In those dogs that do not die from the disease, serious side effects can plague them for the rest of their lives. Unfortunately, as with other viral diseases, there is no specific treatment once a dog becomes infected.

Parvovirus. This virus likes to strike young, unvaccinated puppies under the age of ten weeks, although all ages can be susceptible to infection. It is highly contagious, spreading from dog to dog through oral contamination with infected feces. Parvovirus affects the intestines, causing severe diarrhea and dehydration. In addition, the disease causes immune system depression, leaving the infected dog open to infection by other opportunistic organisms. In some puppies, the heart can be affected by the virus, leading to sudden death due to heart failure.

Infectious Canine Hepatitis (ICH, CAV-1).
Infectious canine hepatitis is found worldwide and is readily transmissible from dog to dog through contact with all types of body excretions, especially the urine. As the name implies, once the organism enters the dog's body, it causes a severe inflammation of the liver, or hepatitis. However, CAV-1 does not stop there. Other organ systems, including the eyes and kidneys, are often attacked as well. Clinical signs of this disease include abdominal pain, jaundice, and internal bleeding. A characteristic lesion of infectious canine hepatitis is called *blue eye*. In this condition, one or both eyes can take on a blue appearance due to fluid buildup and inflammation in the eye(s).

Canine Cough (Parainfluenza). Parainfluenza is a highly contagious respiratory disease, transmitted from dog to dog by air and wind currents contaminated with cough and sneeze

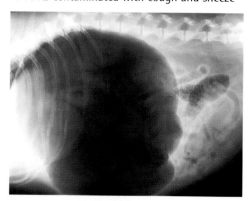

droplets from infected dogs. An instigator of the infamous *canine (kennel) cough complex* that afflicts dogs that are boarded or kept in a kennel environment, it can also rear its ugly head anywhere dogs are congregated, including grooming shops, dog shows, veterinary offices, and so on. The classical clinical sign associated with a parainfluenza infection is a dry, persistent cough.

Parainfluenza is not the only organism that can cause kennel cough. Another important agent is the bacterium *Bordetella bronchiseptica*, which is related to the same bacterium that causes whooping cough in humans. It can result in the most severe form of kennel cough, and can cause permanent damage to the airways if not treated soon enough. An optional intranasal vaccine is available for those dogs spending a lot of time in boarding kennels.

Rabies. Rabies is a deadly viral disease that is transmitted via the saliva of infected animals, usually through a bite wound or contamination of existing open wounds or exposed mucous membranes. Unfortunately, once signs appear, the disease is ultimately fatal.

Dachshunds that are allowed to roam freely or interact with wild animals are at greatest risk of exposure. Rabid dogs can exhibit a variety of clinical signs, from outright dementia and foaming at the mouth to minor behavior changes accompanied by progressive incoordination and paralysis. The only way to definitively diagnose a case of rabies is to have a laboratory analysis performed on the animal's brain tissue, which means of course, euthanasia of the animal in question.

Stomach bloat can be classified as a nutritional disease.

A dividing cancer cell.

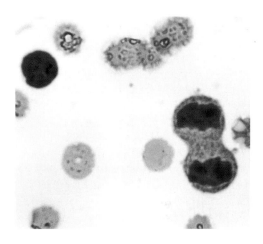

Degenerative Diseases

These diseases include those associated with normal wear and tear due to age, such as certain forms of kidney and heart disease, and those that begin a degenerative course soon after birth. In most cases, degenerative diseases cannot be cured, only managed with the ultimate goal of slowing the degenerative process.

Disk disease: Degenerative disk disease in Dachshunds is caused by a progressive degeneration of the intervertebral disks, those cushion-like structures that separate each vertebra of the spinal column. As the disks degenerate, they calcify and lose their shock-absorbing ability. As a result, the disks so affected become very susceptible to compression damage, even from the normal day-to-day activity. If a sudden or forceful movement occurs, these disks can rupture, oozing their contents into the spinal canal and placing pressure on the spinal cord. Severe or prolonged pressure can lead to paralysis and permanent damage to the spinal cord.

The part of the Dachshund's back most susceptible to rupture is that portion extending from the last rib to the pelvis. The neck region is another highly susceptible area as well. Degenerative disk disease can show up as early as three years of age; however, its incidence increases as Dachshunds grow older. Obese Dachshunds are high-risk candidates for this devastating disorder.

The clinical signs seen when an actual rupture occurs depend on the location of the lesion and the degree of rupture that takes place. Those Dachshunds with mild pressure being exerted on the cord will have pain and be reluctant to move. Many dogs will cry or yelp when picked up. If the neck is involved, any manipulations attempted will be met with vigorous protests. These pets often prefer not to be bothered, and have the tendency to isolate themselves. Appetites are usually reduced as well. Since nerve fibers responsible for coordinated muscle movement run in the outer layers of the spinal cord, owners may also notice weakness and/or incoordination when their Dachshund tries to walk.

With more severe disk ruptures, there can be damage to the deeper portions of the spinal cord. Partial or complete paralysis of one or more limbs might result, again depending on the location of the rupture. In most cases, both hind legs are involved to varying degrees. If the entire depth of the spinal cord is involved, many will also lose all pain sensation in one or all four limbs. Such a severe case carries with it a very grave prognosis, since treatment at this stage is rarely successful.

Diagnosis of degenerative disk disease or disk rupture is made using exam and clinical findings, along with radiographs (X rays) of the vertebral column. A special test called a myelogram may be performed as well, in order to focus in on the exact location of the problem.

The type of treatment that will be prescribed for those Dachshunds suffering from disk disease and/or rupture depends on the extent of the damage done by the disk(s) to the spinal cord. For those dogs exhibiting mild pain with or without slight incoordination, two to four weeks of strict confinement may be indicated. Although antiinflammatories are sometimes used to reduce the swelling and pain, many veterinarians prefer to forego them altogether, since any pain experienced by the affected dog serves to discourage excessive movement and mobility, which, in turn, prevents further damage to the disk and cord until natural healing can take place. Following this rest period, some veterinarians may prescribe physical therapy exercises, including swimming, to help strengthen the back and leg muscles that may have been affected during the episode. If your Dachshund is overweight, rest assured that he will be placed on a strict diet.

For all other cases involving moderate to severe clinical signs, aggressive antiinflammatory drug therapy combined with surgery to remove the affected disk(s), thereby relieving the pressure on the spinal cord, may be the only answer. The clinical signs seen and the radiographic test results will govern such a decision. In severe cases, the sooner the surgery is performed, the greater the chances are for recovery.

In those instances where surgery is unsuccessful and the paralysis is permanent, euthanasia is not always the only option left to the owner. Special "wheelchairs" for Dachshunds paralyzed by intervertebral disk disease are available. Though not for every patient, these carts can help give mobility to select patients willing to wear the apparatus, and provide an option for those owners willing to devote much time and care to their paralyzed pet. If you think such a device could be applicable to your own pet's situation, ask your veterinarian for more details.

Protecting your Dachshund against disk rupture can be done by using specific measures. The first and most important step is to prevent obesity. Although it seems to be inherent to the nature of Dachshunds, jumping on and off furniture or porches should be discouraged. Often, constructing a small ramp to assist your dog' ascents and descents will help ease the burden on the back. Finally, keep in mind that whenever lifting a Dachshund, be sure to firmly support both the front and hind ends as you lift, keeping the back as straight as possible.

Nutritional Diseases

As with humans, nutrition plays a vital—and some say even the number one—role in maintaining healthy organ function, including those making up the immune system. It stands to reason, then, that nutritional deficiencies, whether caused by external or internal factors, can cause devastating disease. Nutritional diseases can also be caused by a malfunctioning digestive system. Disruptions in the body's ability to absorb nutrients from the ration eaten can have the same effects as if the food wasn't eaten at all. Dachshunds that are having difficulty putting on weight, or those that underperform even when fed a high-quality ration should be checked for malabsorption.

Neoplastic Diseases

The term neoplasia refers to the uncontrolled, progressive proliferation of cells in the body. Bypassing the body's normal mechanisms for controlling growth, neoplastic cells reproduce at abnormal rates, often coalescing into firm, distinct masses called tumors. Neoplasia can be classified as either benign or malignant (cancerous), depending on the behavior of the cells involved.

Cancer can present itself as a wide variety of clinical signs and symptoms. Benign neoplasia can cause damage just by sheer size and mechanical disruption; malignant neoplasia can spread throughout the body and affect many organs at once.

Diagnosis of a neoplastic disorder can be accomplished using clinical signs, laboratory testing, radiology, ultrasound, and/or tumor biopsy.

Treatment options for neoplasms include surgical removal of defined tumors, radiation therapy, using ionizing radiation to kill malignant neoplasms, chemotherapy, using specific drugs to destroy neoplastic cells, cryotherapy—freezing tumors to kill neoplastic cells—and immunotherapy—injecting substances in order to stimulate and support the body's immune system in its fight against the tumors—to name a few. A combination of surgery, radiation, and chemotherapy is currently the most favored protocol for treating especially difficult malignancies in dogs. As one may expect, the earlier a cancer is detected, the greater are the chances for complete recovery.

Several different types of neoplasia can affect Dachshunds. One such example is the perianal gland tumor. Perianal gland tumors arise from the glandular tissue surrounding the anal region. They usually present as solitary or multiple irregular masses on or protruding from the skin in or near this area of the body. Because the hormone testosterone influences the growth of these tumors, they are usually seen in older male Dachshunds that have not been neutered. If malignant, metastasis (spread) of the cancer to the surrounding lymph nodes and to distant organs can occur. Diagnosis of perianal gland tumors is made through biopsy evaluation. Treatment involves a combination of surgery, radiation therapy, and castration.

Traumatic/Toxic Disorders

Traumatic disorders include not only those produced by direct, external physical trauma (for example, automobile fenders), but also those produced by toxins or foreign bodies traumatizing the body from within. Automobile-related trauma poses a real health threat to the untrained or poorly trained Dachshund. Also, snakebites, especially on the nose, insect stings, ingested foreign objects, and fight-related trauma can all pose a health threat to the inquisitive or protective pet. Antifreeze is a deadly poison that can cause acute kidney failure if ingested. Its sweet, pleasant taste and smell may actually attract an unsuspecting Dachshund to a spill on the ground!

If you are ever faced with a traumatic or toxic situation involving your Dachshund, don't panic. Contact your veterinarian and/or poison control immediately—in the case of poisoning, don't forget to read the product label for instructions on what to do if poisoning occurs—for instructions.

A Word About Euthanasia

There comes a time when the decision to euthanize a beloved pet must be made. It is a final act of kindness for a seriously ill or injured dog, ending its prolonged suffering and pain.

FIRST AID FOR YOUR DACHSHUND

The ultimate goal of first aid is to assess and stabilize your dog's condition to the best of your ability until you can obtain veterinary assistance. The first item on the agenda is to determine whether or not a life-threatening situation exists. Labored breathing, cessation of breathing or heartbeat, severe bleeding that cannot be stopped with direct pressure, snakebite, dehydration, and poisoning are just a few of the conditions that demand immediate medical attention. Once these serious problems have been addressed, you are then free to direct your attention toward other less serious challenges. Just remember: If your Dachshund is injured or becomes ill, stay calm! Panic will serve no useful purpose and will only hinder your first aid efforts. A little preplanning will help you stay calm in the event of a crisis. First, mentally rehearse these first aid procedures in advance before you ever have to use them. Second, keep the phone numbers of your veterinarian and the nearest veterinary emergency clinic handy in case of emergency. These professionals can walk you through first aid procedures by telephone if you feel you need assistance.

Become familiar with first aid procedures for your Dachshund before you actually need them!

Artificial Respiration/ Cardiopulmonary Resuscitation

The combination of artificial respiration and external heart massage is called *cardiopulmonary resuscitation (CPR)*. Artificial respiration is used to supply oxygen to the lungs and tissues in those instances in which the dog has stopped breathing. If the heart has stopped beating, external heart massage is needed as well to help maintain circulation.

If your Dachshund is unconscious and has stopped breathing:

1. Sweep her mouth with your finger to clear it of any blood, mucus, vomitus, or other debris.

2. Tilt her head back to straighten the airway, then clasp her mouth shut with your hand and place your mouth over your dog's nose and mouth, forming a tight seal.

3. Blow into the nose until you see the chest expand (if a small puppy is involved, deliver gentle puffs of breath to inflate the lungs). If the chest doesn't expand, repeat the first two steps, then try again. If there is still no expansion, probe the back of the throat for a foreign body obstructing the airway.

4. Release the seal, allowing your pet to fully exhale. Deliver three more breaths in rapid succession, then check for a pulse (see HOW-TO: Procedures, page 90).

CHECKLIST

Common Sources of Poisoning

✔ Spoiled or denatured food
✔ Houseplants
✔ Warfarin-based rodent poisons
✔ Cholecalciferol-based rodent poisons
✔ Organophosphate or carbamate insecticides
✔ Metaldehyde-based snail and slug poisons
✔ Arsenic-based insect poisons, weed killers, and wood preservatives
✔ Strychnine-based squirrel, predator, or bird bait
✔ Chocolate (theobromine)
✔ Ethylene glycol (antifreeze)
✔ Ibuprofen
✔ Human prescription medications (anti-depressants; pain relievers, heart medications, and so on)
✔ Lead-based items such as paint, newsprint, linoleum
✔ Zinc-based items such as coins, zinc oxide skin cream, fertilizers
✔ Iron-based garden fertilizers

2. Using a firm, sharp movement, compress the chest about 2 to 3 inches (5–8 cm) with your hands. Each compression should last approximately one-half second. Perform these chest compressions at a rate of one per second.

3. After every five compressions, perform an artificial respiration. Check for a heartbeat after every second cycle.

4. Continue CPR until your pet is breathing on her own or until you can get veterinary care.

Hemorrhage

To control active hemorrhaging, apply direct pressure over the source of the bleeding using any absorbent material or object available, such as a shirt, towel, or gauze. For minor bleeding, maintain this pressure with your hands for a good five minutes before releasing. For major hemorrhaging, including those instances where blood spurts from the wound, indicating a damaged artery, secure the compress tightly over the wound using gauze, a belt, pantyhose, or a necktie, and seek veterinary help immediately. If an extremity is involved, pressure applied to the inside, upper portion of the affected leg near its attachment to the body will also reduce blood flow to the limb.

5. Repeat this sequence once every three seconds until your dog is breathing on her own, or until you can get veterinary assistance.

If no pulse is detected, institute external heart massage.

1. Start by administering three more breaths in rapid succession, then lay your dog on her right side and place the heel of one hand on her rib cage just behind the elbow. Place your other hand on top of the first.

Poisoning

General symptoms associated with poisoning include vomiting, diarrhea, unconsciousness, seizures, abdominal pain, excessive salivation, panting, and/or shock.

The treatment aim for poisoning is to eliminate, dilute, or neutralize the poison as quickly as possible prior to veterinary intervention. If the poison came from a container, read and follow the label directions concerning accidental poisoning. Be sure to take the label and container with you to your veterinarian.

Treatment

If your Dachshund has ingested a caustic or petroleum-based substance, or is severely depressed, seizuring, or unconscious, waste no time in seeking veterinary help. Treatment in these instances should be administered only under a veterinarian's guidance.

For other poisons that were eaten, induce vomiting using 1 teaspoon per 10 pounds (4.5 kg) of body weight of hydrogen peroxide or 1/2 ml per pound syrup of ipecac. Repeat the dosage of hydrogen peroxide in five minutes if needed.

Once the dog vomits, administer two cups of water orally to help dilute any remaining poison. If available, administer activated charcoal (mix 25 grams of powder in water to form a slurry, then administer one ml per pound of body weight) or whole milk (one cup) to help deactivate any residual poison. Then take your dog to your veterinarian immediately.

If the poison was applied to the skin, flush the affected areas with copious amounts of water. If the offending substance is oil-based, a quick bath using water plus a mechanics' hand cleaner or dishwashing liquid should be performed to remove any remaining residue.

In all instances of poisoning, specific antidotes may be available at your veterinarian's office. As a result, always seek out professional care following initial first aid efforts.

Paralysis

Certainly the most common cause of paralysis in Dachshunds is one or more ruptured intervertebral disks along the back. Unfortunately, there are no specific first aid measures you can institute at home other than keeping your dog calm and preventing further movement. Time is of the essence here; don't delay in seeking veterinary help. When picking up your dog for transport, keep her back as straight as possible. Ideally, use a solid support such as a piece of plywood or sturdy window screen on which to transport her to your veterinarian.

Fractures

Bone fractures are characterized by abnormal limb position or mobility, localized pain, bruising, and/or crepitation, the crackling that can be felt when two ends of bone are rubbed together. If bone is protruding through the skin, do not attempt to replace it or clean the wound. Control any bleeding and apply a clean or sterile bandage to the site prior to transporting your dog to the veterinarian. If you suspect that a limb fracture has occurred below the elbow or knee, try to immobilize the limb by applying a splint to the affected region. Tongue depressors, emery boards, rulers, bubble wrap used for shipping, and other rigid items around the house can be affixed to the limb with adhesive tape or cloth and used as makeshift splints. Be careful not to apply any tape directly over the fracture site. Once the fracture is splinted, carefully transport your Dachshund to the veterinarian at once for further stabilization.

Allergic Reactions

Allergic reactions in Dachshunds can occur secondary to such things as vaccinations, insect stings, or the administration of oral medications.

Reactions can appear within minutes to hours following exposure to the offending agent. Mild reactions are characterized by facial swelling, itching, hives, and localized soreness. Moderate reactions can involve these signs, as well as prolonged vomiting, diarrhea, fever, and lethargy. Severe allergic reactions are characterized by breathing difficulties, severe vomiting and/or diarrhea, shock, collapse, and unconsciousness.

If your Dachshund experiences an allergic reaction, regardless of severity, seek veterinary assistance immediately. For mild reactions, you can administer diphenhydramine orally at a dosage of one milligram per pound of body weight prior to or during the trip to the veterinary hospital. If the reaction is mild and was caused by something you put on the dog's skin and haircoat, wash her off to remove as much of the offending substance as possible prior to transport. However, if your pet is undergoing a severe reaction, don't delay in transporting her to the veterinarian. Keep her as calm as possible, and if the reaction is severe, render cardiopulmonary resuscitation if needed.

Be prepared in case of accident!

Vomiting and Diarrhea

Any irritation involving the digestive tract can lead to bouts of vomiting and diarrhea. Common causes in young Dachshunds include— but are not limited to—dietary indiscretions, intestinal parasites, and viral diseases, whereas common causes in adults include foreign bodies, metabolic diseases (such as kidney disease), pancreatitis, and, again, dietary indiscretions.

Dehydration

Both vomiting and diarrhea can quickly lead to a state of dehydration. Dehydration in itself places a tremendous strain on the internal organs, and can lead to circulatory shock and organ failure if not managed aggressively. Also, keep in mind that Dachshund puppies can dehydrate seven times faster than adult animals. As a result, any signs of dehydration in a young dog should be especially regarded as a medical emergency.

One way to determine your pet's hydration status is to check the skin elasticity. Gently grasp the skin on top of your pet's neck, lift it up, then release it. If it fails to return to its normal position within two seconds, then your pet is severely dehydrated. Keep in mind that some dehydrated pets can have normal skin elasticity, so don't be lulled into a false sense of security by this procedure.

Simply allowing a dehydrated pet unlimited access to water will not correct the condition, since little will be absorbed into the body through the irritated bowel walls. Instead, intravenous fluids and/or colloids will be required to correct the condition.

Treatment

For mild cases of stomach upset in an adult
Dachshund, where no more than one or two
episodes of vomiting occur, bismuth subsalicy-
late can be administered at a dosage rate
of one teaspoon per 5 pounds (2 kg) of body
weight. The same dosage can be administered
to those dogs with diarrhea that are alert
and otherwise acting healthy. However, if
your dog becomes depressed, vomits more
than two times, seems to have pain in the
abdomen, has diarrhea along with vomiting,
has blood in the stool, or has diarrhea lasting
longer than 48 hours, take her to your veterinarian before you administer anything at
home.

*A Dachshund suffering from an upset
stomach will often be reluctant to move.*

Seizures

Seizures are characterized by an alteration
in mental acuity and/or involuntary rapid
muscle contraction. Causes of seizures in
Dachshunds can include idiopathic epilepsy,
poisoning, organ failure, elevated body temperature, tumors, low blood calcium, seen in
pregnant and nursing mothers, and low blood
sugar, seen in young puppies. If your pet
experiences a seizure, don't panic! Simply wrap
her in a thick blanket or towel to prevent her
from hurting herself. If your pet has been
previously diagnosed as having epilepsy, your
veterinarian may prescribe medication to be
given at home per rectum in the event of a
seizure episode. If your pet has never experienced a seizure before, take her to your veterinarian for laboratory tests to determine the
underlying cause and for appropriate preventive treatment.

HOW-TO: PROCEDURES

Taking Your Dog's Temperature

To take your dog's temperature, lubricate the tip of a plastic digital thermometer with a water-soluble lubricant. Do not use glass thermometers, as these can break and damage your pet's rectum. Insert the digital thermometer into the rectum and hold it in place until the thermometer's beeper goes off. Normal temperature should fall somewhere between 99.5 and 102.5°F (37.5–39.2°C). Elevated temperatures can be caused by increased physical activity, high environmental temperatures, inflammation, and/or infection. If your dog's temperature reading is higher than 102.5°F, and your dog seems lethargic or showing signs of illness, call your veterinarian for advice.

Taking a Pulse

You can take your pet's pulse in one of several different ways. The first is to place your fingertips on your pet's chest just behind the point of the elbow, press inward, and feel for the heartbeat. Another area in which to feel for a pulse is in the groin region, or more specifically, in the middle of the inner portion of either leg, just below its junction with the abdomen. A third location would be on either side of the trachea, in the groove formed by the trachea and the muscles of the neck. Keeping an eye on your watch, simply count the number of pulses or heartbeats you detect over a 20-second period, then multiply this number by three to obtain a per minute rate. The normal range for Dachshunds is 80 to 120 beats per minute.

Obtaining a Respiratory Rate

To measure your dog's respiratory rate, simply observe the rise and fall of her rib cage as she breathes. Count the number of breaths taken over a 15-second interval, then multiply that figure by

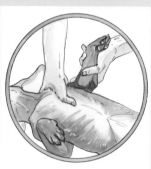

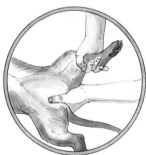

Checking the pulse.

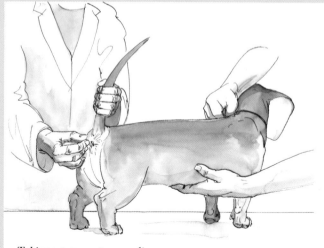

Taking a temperature reading.

four. Of course, respiratory rates are difficult to obtain if the dog is panting. The normal respiratory rate for a calm Dachshund should range between 12 and 30 breaths per minute.

Administering Oral Tablets and Liquids

To administer a tablet to your Dachshund, start by lubricating the tablet with a small dab of butter. Open your pet's mouth by placing your hand over her top jaw, with your thumb and fingers situated behind the upper canine teeth. Now tilt the head back, and press inward and upward with your thumb and fingers. This will cause your pet to open her mouth. Next, with the fingers of your free hand, which is holding the pill, pull down gently on the lower jaw and place the pill far back on the center of the tongue, using your fingers or better yet, a commercial pet-piller. Close your Dachshund's mouth and gently stroke her throat to encourage her to swallow the pill.

To administer oral liquids, first hook your finger between the skin at the corner of the mouth and the teeth and "tent" the skin of the cheek out away from the gum line. Insert the syringe, dropper, or spoon into the pocket formed. Pointing your pet's muzzle at a 45-degree angle, deliver the medication slowly. Gently stroke the throat to encourage swallowing. Do not put a liquid medication directly onto the tongue or into the back of the throat, as your pet may choke on it.

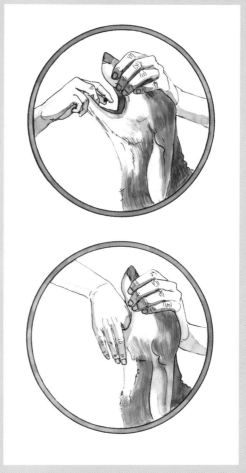

Administering a pill to a Dachshund.

BREEDING AND SHOWING YOUR DACHSHUND

Breeding: Think Twice

The decision on whether or not to breed your Dachshund is not one to be taken lightly. To be certain you are making the correct decision, the following two considerations should always be addressed.

1. As any professional dog breeder will attest to, producing top-quality Dachshunds takes a considerable investment both in terms of time and money.

Maintaining genetic integrity and impeccable standards of care, regardless of investment involved, is always first and foremost in the mind of the ethical breeder. If you are not a professional breeder and want to breed your Dachshund to produce a source of income for yourself or to allow your children to experience the miracle of life, it's best to rethink your decision. Many amateur breeders quickly discover that the costs associated with bringing a new litter into the world can far exceed the income derived from such an experience. Of course, there are those unethical individuals who will ultimately decline to seek out medical help for a sick mother or newborn or will breed the dog even though it harbors an obvious defect (see page 75 for a listing of some of the

Dachshunds are natural-born competitors.

more common inherited diseases that affect Dachshunds). But since you are not one of these individuals, this of course does not apply to you!

2. Will your decision to breed your dog serve to advance the breed? For instance, if your dog happens to be an excellent competitor in the show ring or has an exceptional personality, passing these qualities on to future generations may be well worth the commitment required. If not, it is best for the breed's sake not to allow your dog to reproduce.

If you wish to obtain a genetically similar successor to your current Dachshund, there is an option available to you. Consider contacting the original breeder from whom you purchased your existing friend. He or she will no doubt still own breeding dogs that are related to yours, or if not, can help you trace and locate relatives of your dog that are still used for breeding purposes and can be used to produce a puppy that shares common genes with your dog.

Don't be fearful about neutering your Dachshund if you decide not to breed it. The health benefits neutering affords your dog are tremendous, and many of the myths that exist about this procedure are simply not true. For more information on neutering, see Neutering Your Dachshund, page 68.

A typical whelping box.

Checking for Inherited Disorders

Once you fully understand the responsibilities that go along with breeding your Dachshund, and you still wish to proceed with it, the next step is to check your dog's pedigree closely back at least two generations to search for inherited disorders that his or her ancestors may have had. This involves contacting the owners of your dog's parents and grandparents, whether or not these relatives are still living, and inquiring about their dog's health and personality. Remember that genetic disorders often skip generations, and even though your dog showed no obvious signs of such defects, his or her offspring very well could. Obviously, if there is indeed a history of inherited diseases in your dog's pedigree, he or she should not be used for breeding purposes.

Stud Dogs

If you own a female Dachshund and need to arrange a stud dog for her, look for one with a pleasant personality and good conformational qualities. Inquire at your local breed association for recommendations regarding quality stud dogs in your area. Avoid choosing a dog with the same bloodline as yours in order to prevent complications associated with inbreeding.

Finally, prior to embarking on this adventure, acquaint yourself with the basic principles of canine reproduction and neonatal care in order to ensure smooth sailing. There are many excellent resources, including a number of useful books and web sites, available to teach you these principles. Talk to your veterinarian as well as to experienced Dachshund breeders to get a feel about what to expect and to amass as many tips as you can. Remember that the more educated you become, the more comfortable you will be with the overall process. Here's a great tip to get you started: Because reputable breeders ultimately take responsibility for every puppy their dogs bring into the world, consider advertising your puppies for sale even before you begin the breeding process. That way, you can screen for good homes for the new puppies before they are even born. Also, offer a discount off the purchase price in return for a refundable deposit to "hold" a puppy for a potential buyer.

The Competitive Dachshund

For many, the thrill of competition will lead them to enter their four-legged companions into one of the many competitive events that take place throughout the country every year.

The majority of these events are sanctioned and administered by the American Kennel Club (AKC), which has adopted bylaws, regulations, and rules that govern them.

Formal or licensed events are events in which points are earned toward championship titles. To win such a title will not only fill you with a sense of pride, but can also make your Dachshund more valuable for breeding purposes. In addition to formal events, match trials are also held. No points are earned during these trials; instead, dogs compete for fun for ribbons, trophies, and other awards. Match trials are held regularly by local breed clubs and all-breed obedience clubs. Such events are great places to start for the aspiring competitor.

Six types of events that are popular among Dachshund owners and their dogs include dog shows, obedience trials, Dachshund field trials, earthdog tests, tracking tests, and agility competitions. Before entering your Dachshund in a specific event, first do your homework. Attend as many of those events as possible as a spectator in order to acquaint yourself with the procedures and rules. Go to these armed with your questions, and get them answered by networking with the Dachshund owners who have entered their dogs in the competition for that day. Ask for recommendations of any books, literature, publications, Internet addresses, electronic mailboxes, and/or chat rooms that could serve to further enhance your knowledge on the subject. Obviously, the more information you can gather prior to your dog becoming an actual contestant, the better the chances are for success for you and your dog when your time comes to compete.

Find out about the dates and locations of events in your area by contacting local breed-

CHECKLIST

Costs Associated with Responsible Breeding
✔ Pre-breeding health exam
✔ Stud fees
✔ Prenatal care
✔ Veterinary fees resulting from whelping complications
✔ Puppy food
✔ Puppy health exams
✔ Vaccinations
✔ Dewormings
✔ Advertising
✔ Veterinary fees in the event one or more of the puppies becomes ill

ers, veterinarians, trainers, and Dachshund clubs. The AKC will also be able to provide you with listings of competitions in your area. As you might expect, the Internet will also provide a wealth of information regarding these competitions (see Information, page 100, for addresses).

The Events

When a dog is entered in a dog show, it is judged on how closely it conforms to its breed's conformational and physical standard, as established by the national breed club (for the most current standard, contact the AKC at www.akc.org or the Dachshund Club of America, Inc. at www.Dachshund-dca.org). In order for your dog to compete in such a show, it must be sexually intact and must not harbor

Dachshunds and their owners enjoying the thrill of competition.

Before deciding to breed your Dachshund, understand all of the resources necessary to do it responsibly.

any characteristics that may disqualify it, according to the breed standard (see the standard on page 7).

Specialty and Group Shows

Dog shows come in several varieties. The first type of dog show is called a *specialty show*. This show is an intrabreed (one-breed) competition, usually put on by the breed's national parent club or local regional club. A second type is a *group show*, which consists of a competitive gathering of dogs that all belong to the same AKC grouping. Still a third type of dog show is the *all-breed show*, in which multiple breeds from different AKC groups compete together. Many of these shows are held in conjunction with one another. Judging is based on the process of elimination, with the overall winner being crowned Best in Show.

Obedience Trials

The obedience trial is another type of competition in which you can enter your Dachshund. In these events, dogs are led through a series of exercises and commands, with judges scoring their performances along the way. There are multiple levels or titles that dogs compete for in obedience trials, with the ultimate goal of becoming Obedience Trial Champion. Each dog-handler team starts out with a set number of points, then points are deducted for slowness, lack of attention, and/or vocalization. In fact, if a handler must repeat a command, the team is automatically disqualified.

In contrast to dog shows, scoring in obedience trials has nothing to do with physical conformation. In fact, dogs that have been neutered or have other physical defects are still welcome to compete in these events; however, all four-legged contestants must be at least six months old to enter.

Field Trials

For serious enthusiasts, field trials offer a chance to test the innate abilities and skills of their dogs to perform the original functions that the breed was intended to perform. As a breed, Dachshunds compete in their own special field trials. Member field trials are events put on by Dachshund clubs that are members of the American Kennel Club. Licensed field trials, on the other hand, are held by clubs that are not members of the American Kennel Club, but have obtained special licensing from the AKC to hold the field trial event. In both member and licensed field trials, individual Dachshunds can be awarded championship points. A third type of field trial, the sanctioned field trial, is an informal event in which dogs may compete but cannot earn championship points. These trials, too, are sanctioned by the American Kennel Club. For further information regarding rules and regulations for these events, contact the Dachshund Club of America or the AKC directly or via their web sites (see Information, page 100).

Dachshund field trials are run on either rabbits or hares. Classes include Open All Age Dogs and Open All Age Bitches. First, second, third, and fourth place prizes are awarded in each class. In order to earn the coveted title of Field Champion, a Dachshund must stand out from the crowd in searching ability, pursuing ability, accuracy in trailing game, obedience to commands given, properly timed vocalizations, endurance, courage and determination, patience, adaptability to changes in scenting and environmental conditions, independence, cooperation with others, and competitive drive.

Impulsive or erratic behavior is considered faulty by the judges. Those dogs exhibiting intelligence, enthusiasm, and persistence in the hunt ultimately win.

Earthdog Tests

Special types of field events, called earthdog tests, are designed to test the Dachshund's willingness to "go to ground" after game. Contestants are required to navigate through various tunnels and pipes, simulating the original function of the breed, that is, to follow their quarry into and flush them out of underground lairs. Dachshunds must be at least six months of age to enter earthdog competitions.

Tracking Tests

Tracking tests are also exciting competitive events for Dachshunds. These competitions are designed to measure the ability of the individual competitors to follow a scent.

Agility Competitions

In agility competitions, dogs are guided by their owners over a course filled with, among other things, obstacles they must jump over, tires and tunnels they must go through, and poles they must weave in and out of. These are timed events, measuring agility under pressure. Penalties are assessed if obstacles are missed or knocked down, or if time runs out before the course is finished. As with other types of competitive events, various levels of proficiency receive awards, from the most basic to the most advanced agility talents. Your Dachshund must be at least one year of age to enter these competitions.

Dachshund Events—A Recap

There are six types of events popular among Dachshund owners and their dogs. These competitive events are held throughout the year and most are sanctioned and administered by the AKC. Before entering your Dachshund in any of these events, attend as many competitions as possible. Ask questions and get recommendations from other owners who have entered their Dachshunds in these events.

✔ **Dog shows.** These events judge how well a dog conforms to the breed standard as established by the national breed club.

✔ **Obedience trials.** These competitions lead a dog through a series of exercises and commands, with judges scoring its performance along the way.

✔ **Field trials.** Field trials test the innate abilities and skills of the breed to perform its original function. These functions include hunting, retrieving, etc.

✔ **Earthdog tests.** These are special types of field trials designed to test a Dachshund's willingness to pursue quarry and flush them out of underground lairs.

✔ **Tracking tests.** These tests measure a dog's ability to follow a scent.

✔ **Agility competitions.** These competitions lead dogs and their owners over a course filled with obstacles. Contestants are timed, and penalties are assessed for any missed obstacles.

INFORMATION

Associations

American Boarding Kennel Association
4575 Galley Road, Suite 400-A
Colorado Springs, CO 80915

American Humane Association
9725 East Hampton Avenue
Denver, CO 80231

American Kennel Club
260 Madison Avenue
New York, NY 10016
For Registration, Records, Litter Information:
5580 Centerview Drive
Raleigh, NC 27606

American Veterinary Medical Association
930 North Meacham Road
Schaumburg, IL 60173

Canadian Kennel Club
111 Eglington Avenue
Toronto 12, Ontario
Canada

Canine Eye Registry Foundation (CERF)
South Campus Court, Building C
West Lafayette, IN 47907

Institute for Genetic Disease Control (GDC)
P.O. Box 222
Davis, CA 95617

Kennel Club, The
1-4 Clargis Street
Picadilly
London W7Y8AB
England

Morris Animal Foundation
45 Inverness Drive East
Englewood, CO 80112-5480

National Dog Registry (tattoo, microchip)
P.O. Box 116
Woodstock, NY 12498

Orthopedic Foundation for Animals (OFA)
2300 Nifong Boulevard
Columbia, MO 65201

Owner-Handler Association of America
583 Knoll Court
Seaford, NY 11783

Tattoo-A-Pet
Department 1625
Emmons Avenue
Brooklyn, NY 11235

Books

Ackerman, Lowell and Gary Landsberg. *Dog Behavior and Training: Veterinary Advice for Owners.* Neptune, NJ: TFH Publications, 1996.

Coile, D. Caroline. *Barron's Encyclopedia of Dog Breeds.* Hauppauge, NY: Barron's Educational Series, Inc., 1998.

Griffin, James and Lisa Carlson. *The Dog Owner's Home Veterinary Handbook.* Foster City, CA: IDG Books Worldwide, 1999.

Hornsby, Alison. *Barron's All About Training.* Hauppauge, NY: Barron's Educational Series, Inc., 1999.

Pinney, Chris C. *Caring For Your Older Dog.* Hauppauge, NY: Barron's Educational Series, Inc., 1995.

Web Sites

American Kennel Club	*www.akc.org*
American Veterinary Medical Association	*www.avma.org*
Dachshund Club of America, Inc.	*www.dachshund-dca.org*
Dog Fancy	*www.dogfancy.com*
Waltham World of Pet Care	*www.waltham.com*

Periodicals

AKC Gazette
51 Madison Avenue
New York, NY 10010

Dog Fancy
P.O. Box 53264
Boulder, CO 80322-3264

Dog World
29 North Wacker Drive
Chicago, IL 60606

Gaines Touring with Towser
P.O. Box 5700
Kankakee, IL 60902

Photo Credits

Isabelle Francais: pages 2-3, 4, 8, 20, 21, 24 top, 28, 33 bottom, 36, 44 bottom, 45 right, 52, 53 top left, 53 bottom, 56, 64, 68, 97 top, 97 bottom; Bonnie Nance: pages 12 bottom left, 13 top right, 53 top right, 69 bottom, 40, 44 top, 61 bottom, 64 top right, 65 left, 65 right, 69 top, 72, 96 top left; Judith Strom: pages 24 bottom, 45 left, 96 top right, 96 bottom left, 96 bottom right; Norvia Behling: pages 12 top left, 13 bottom right, 25 top, 25 bottom, 32 top, 32 bottom, 33 top, 48, 77, 88, 89; Pets by Paulette: pages 12 bottom right, 13 top left, 13 bottom left, 84, 92, 101; Toni Tucker: page 16; Daniel Johnson: page 41; Chris Pinney: pages 61 top, 64 top left, 76, 80, 81.

Cover Credits

Kent and Donna Dannen.

Important Note

This pet owner's guide tells the reader how to buy and care for a Dachshund. The author and the publisher consider it important to point out that the advice given in the book is meant primarily for normally developed puppies from a good breeder—that is, dogs of excellent physical health and good character.

Anyone who adopts a fully grown dog should be aware that the animal has already formed its basic impressions of human beings. The new owner should watch the animal carefully, including its behavior toward humans, and should meet the previous owner. If the dog comes from a shelter, it may be possible to get some information on the dog's background and peculiarities there. There are dogs that as a result of bad experiences with humans behave in an unnatural manner or may even bite. Only people that have experience with dogs should take in such an animal.

Caution is further advised in the association of children with dogs, in meetings with other dogs, and in exercising the dog without a leash.

Even well-behaved and carefully supervised dogs sometimes do damage to someone else's property or cause accidents. It is, therefore, in the owner's interest to be adequately insured against such eventualities, and we strongly urge all dog owners to purchase a liability policy that covers their dog.

To Alexandra, Hunter, and Dakota

About the Author

Dr. Chris C. Pinney is a practicing veterinarian and author of seven books, including *Caring For Your Older Dog* and the award-winning *Caring For Your Older Cat,* both published by Barron's Educational Series, Inc. Dr. Pinney has also appeared on numerous radio and television programs across the country, promoting pet health care. He currently resides in Schulenburg, Texas with his wife, children, and numerous four-legged friends!

All inquiries should be addressed to:
Barron's Educational Series, Inc.
250 Wireless Boulevard
Hauppauge, NY 11788
http://www.barronseduc.com

International Standard Book No. 0-7641-1247-3

Library of Congress Catalog Card No. 00-023598

Library of Congress Cataloging-in-Publication Data
Pinney, Chris C.
    Dachshunds : everything about purchase, care, nutrition, behavior, and training / Chris Pinney.
      p. cm. (A Complete pet owner's manual)
    Includes bibliographical references (p.).
    ISBN 0-7641-1247-3 (alk. paper)
    1. Dachshunds. I. Title. II. Series.
SF429.D25 P56   2000
636.753'8—dc21   00-023598

Printed in Hong Kong

9 8 7 6 5 4 3